Copyright © 2024 by Krystal M. Frenchwood for M3llow_K
Editor: Alonzo D. Archibald
ISBN:978-1-7362568-9-3

All rights reserved. This coloring book and any original sketches by Krystal Frenchwood may not be reproduced, sold, claimed or reprin in whole or in part, in any form, by any means, electronic, mechani photocopying or other without permission.

Published by M3llow_K
6608 Gulf Freeway South Ste 600
#128, La Marque, TX 77568

For more details or ordering information, contact the publisher at m3llowk@gmail.com

Hey lovebug! Thank you for continuing to stay tuned into the ow_K vibe! Our new coloring book helps **_Awaken Your Supernova ams_** and illustrates how we all have our own unique abilities or ills (superpowers) and can utilize them to leave an impact by changing the world. In this coloring book it includes positive mations. You can unlock and discover your dreams or passions that lie deep inside of you.

Supernova Dreams
Coloring Book
By: Krystal M. Frenchwood

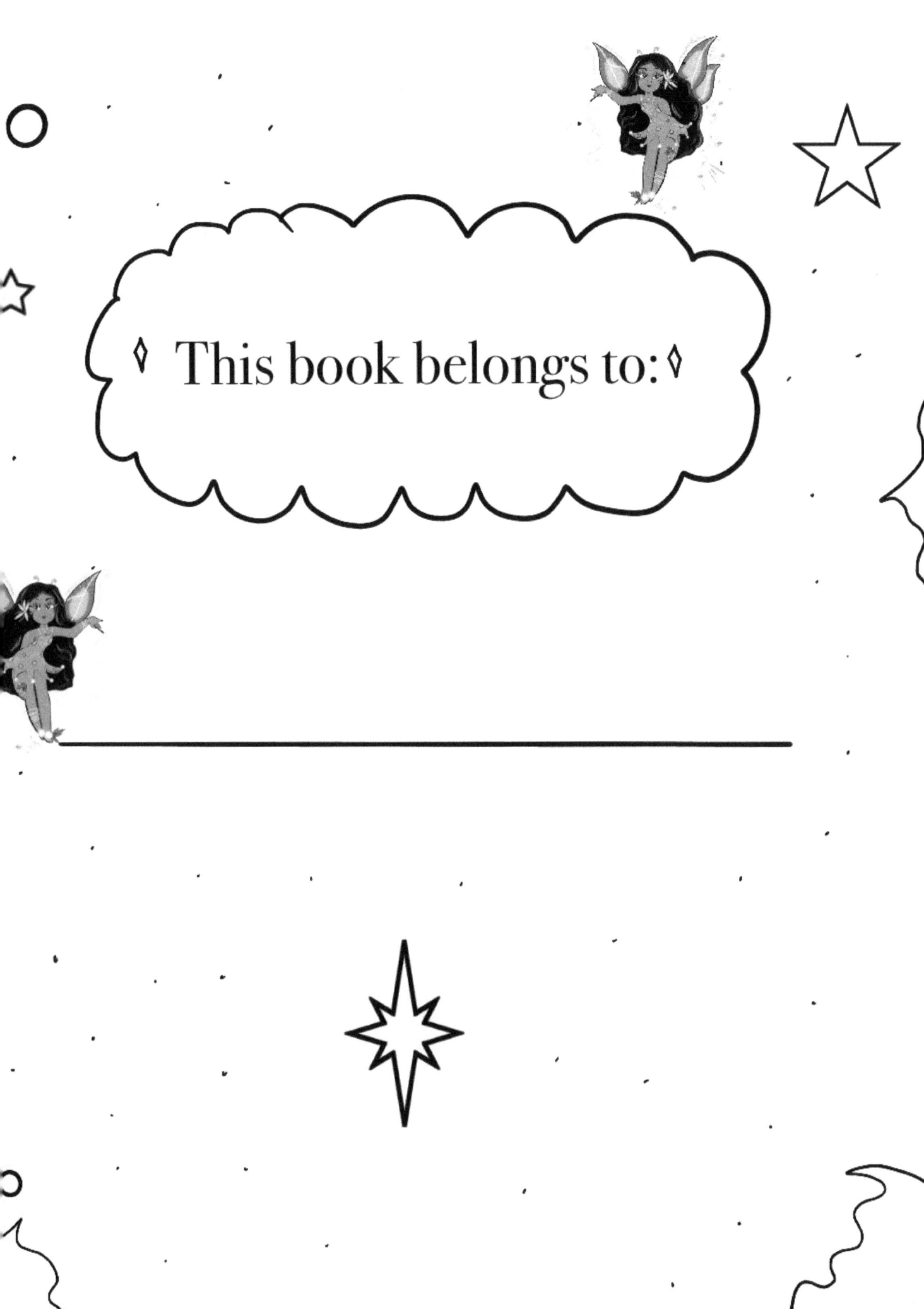

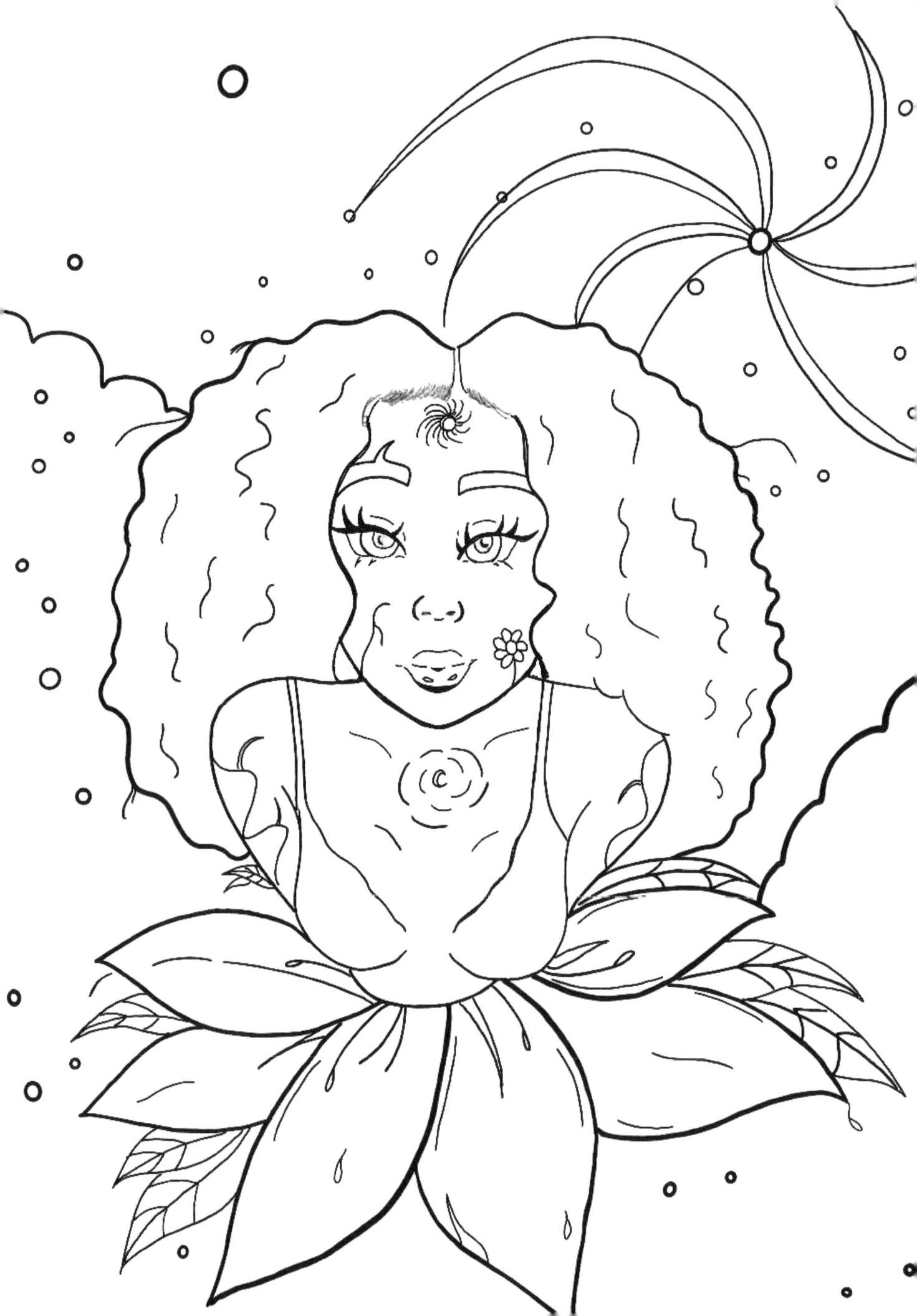

Following my heart

Stay true to you!

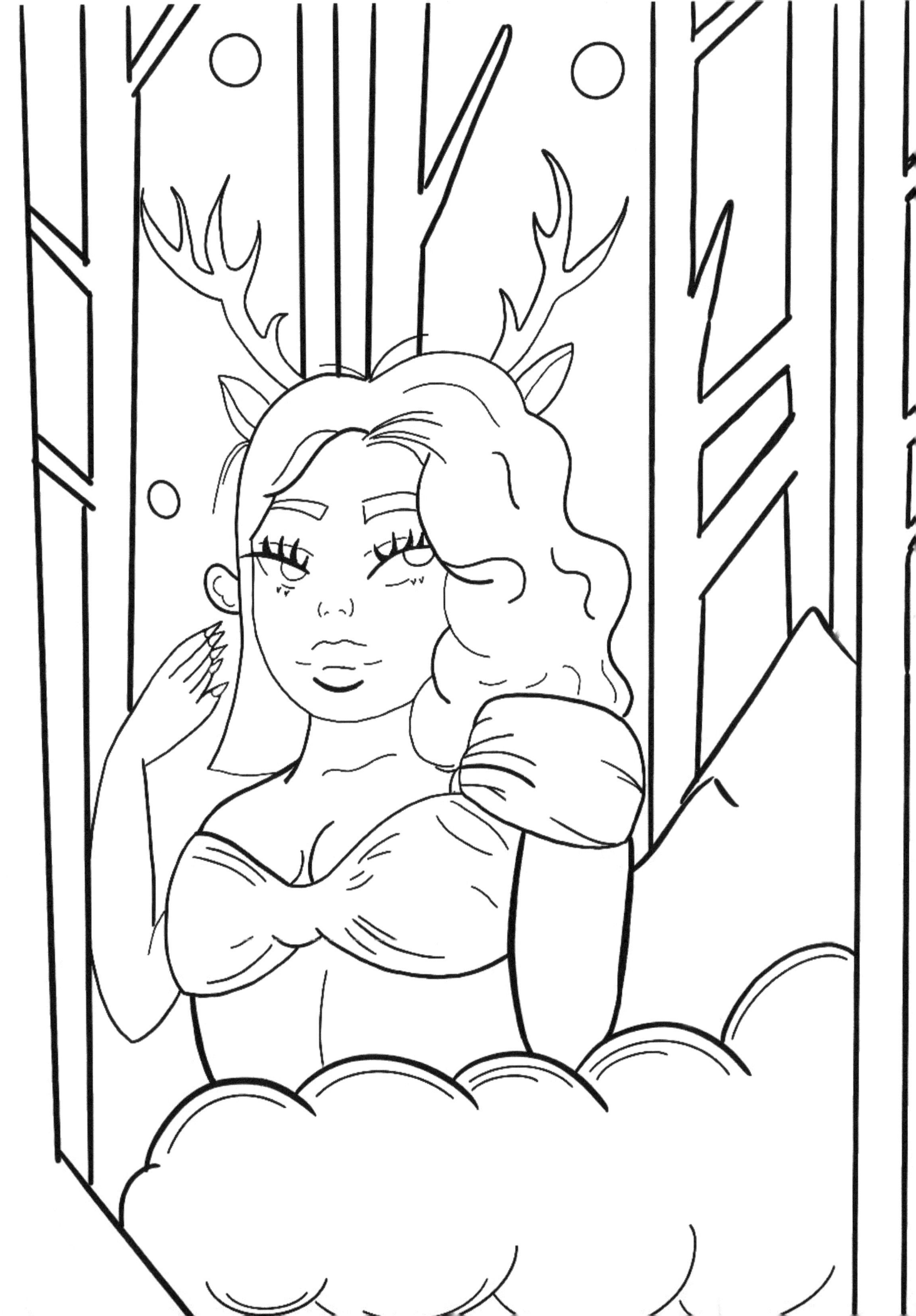

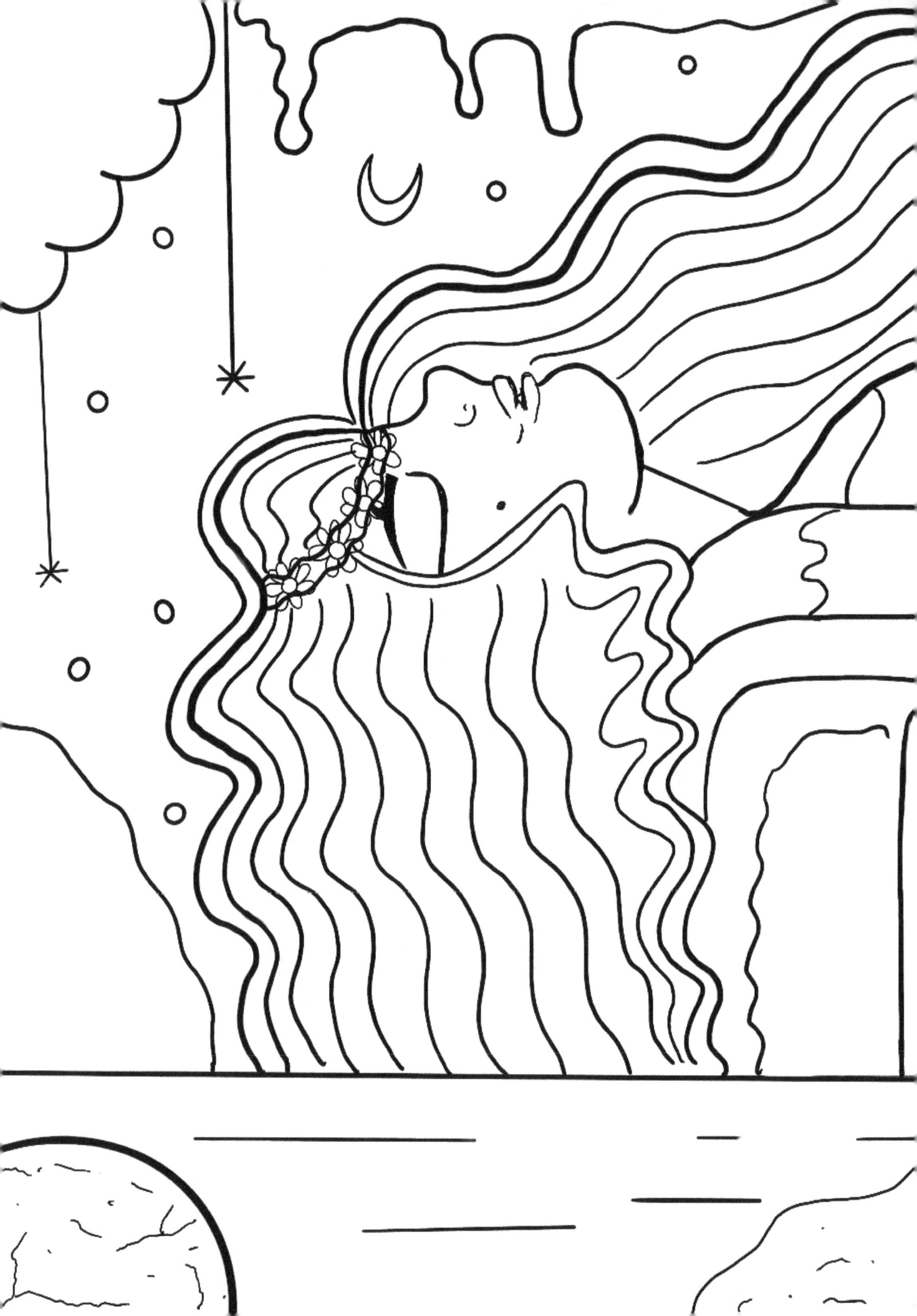

I am amazing!

I am special!

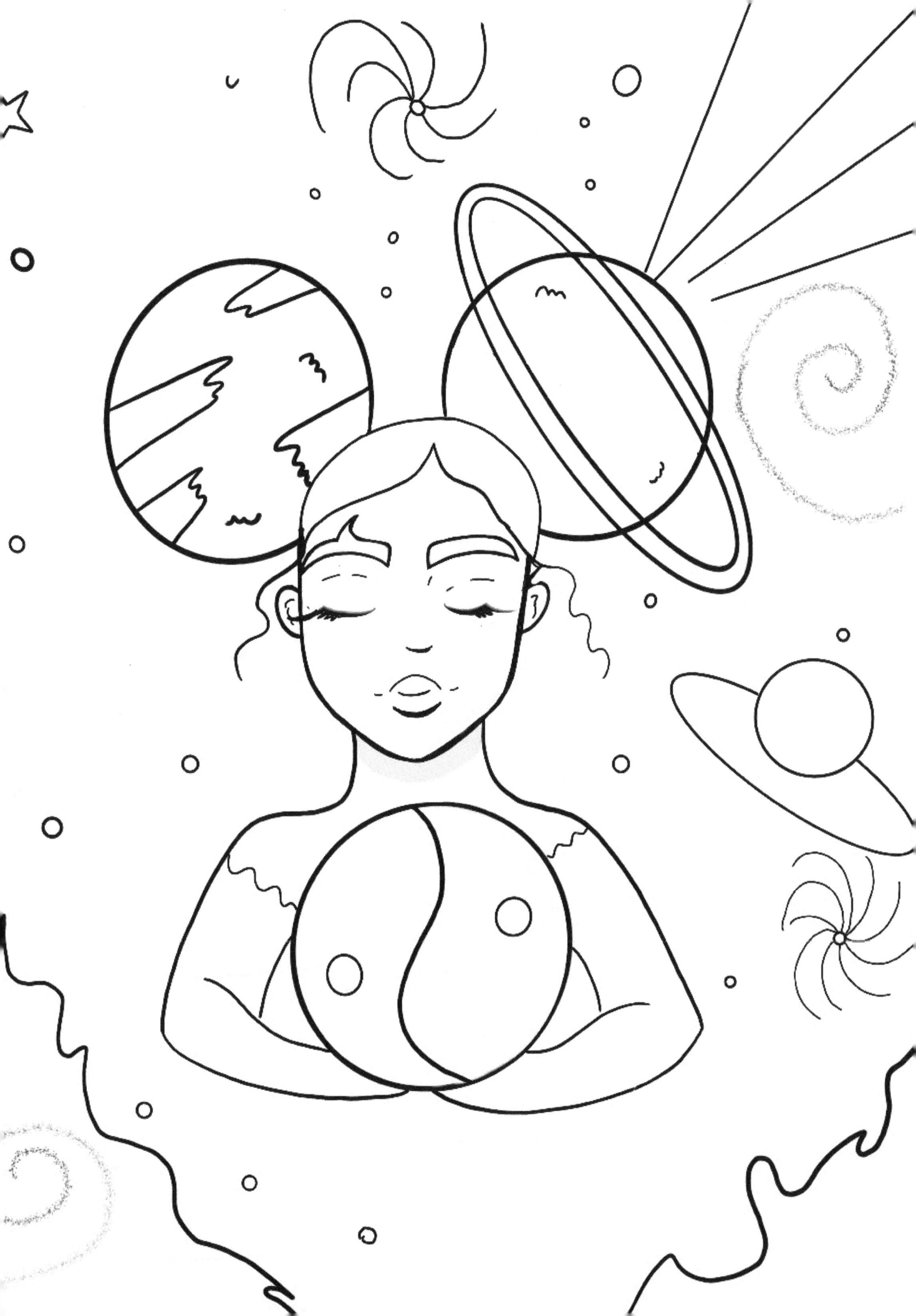

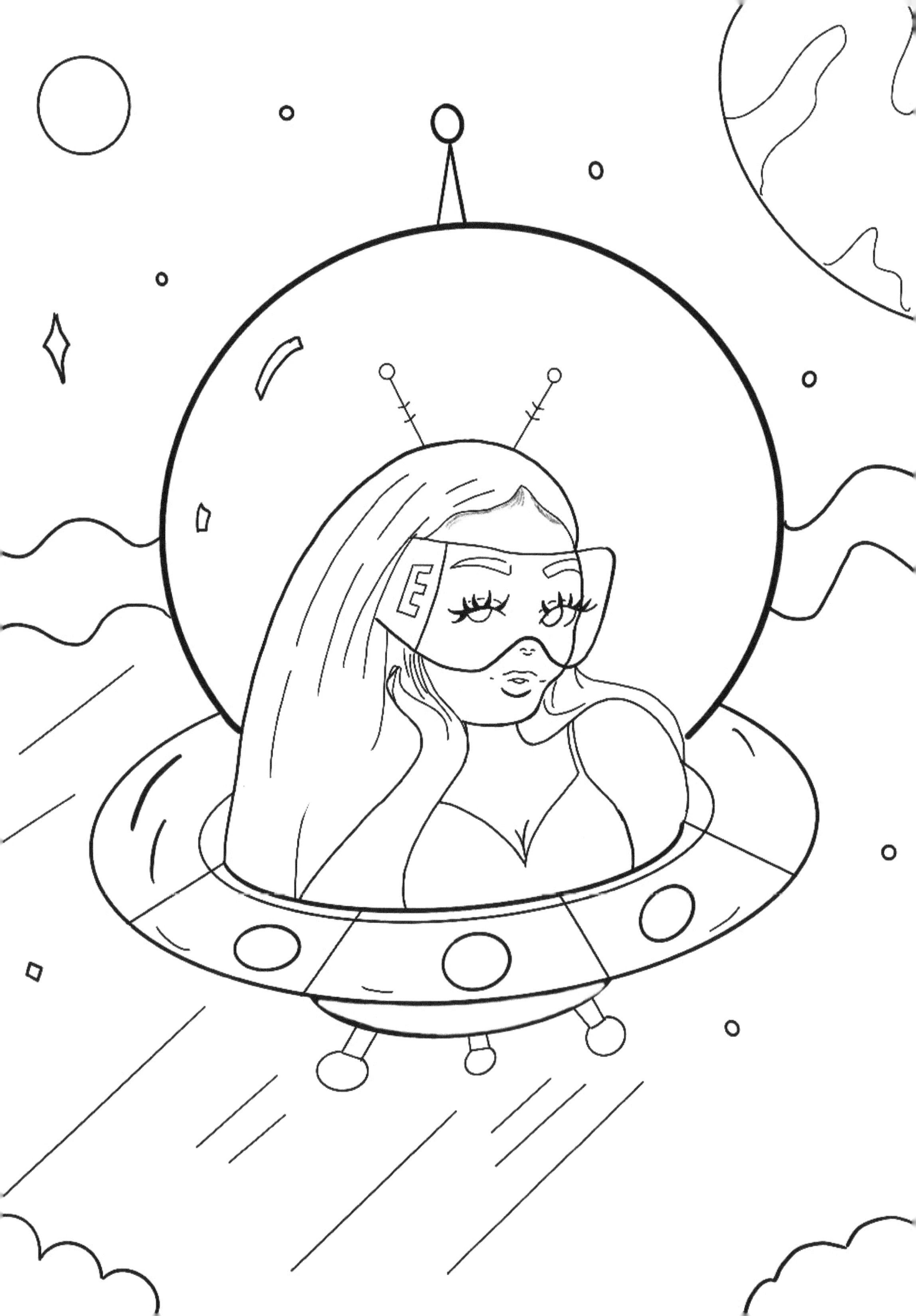

I am adventurous!

I am fearless!

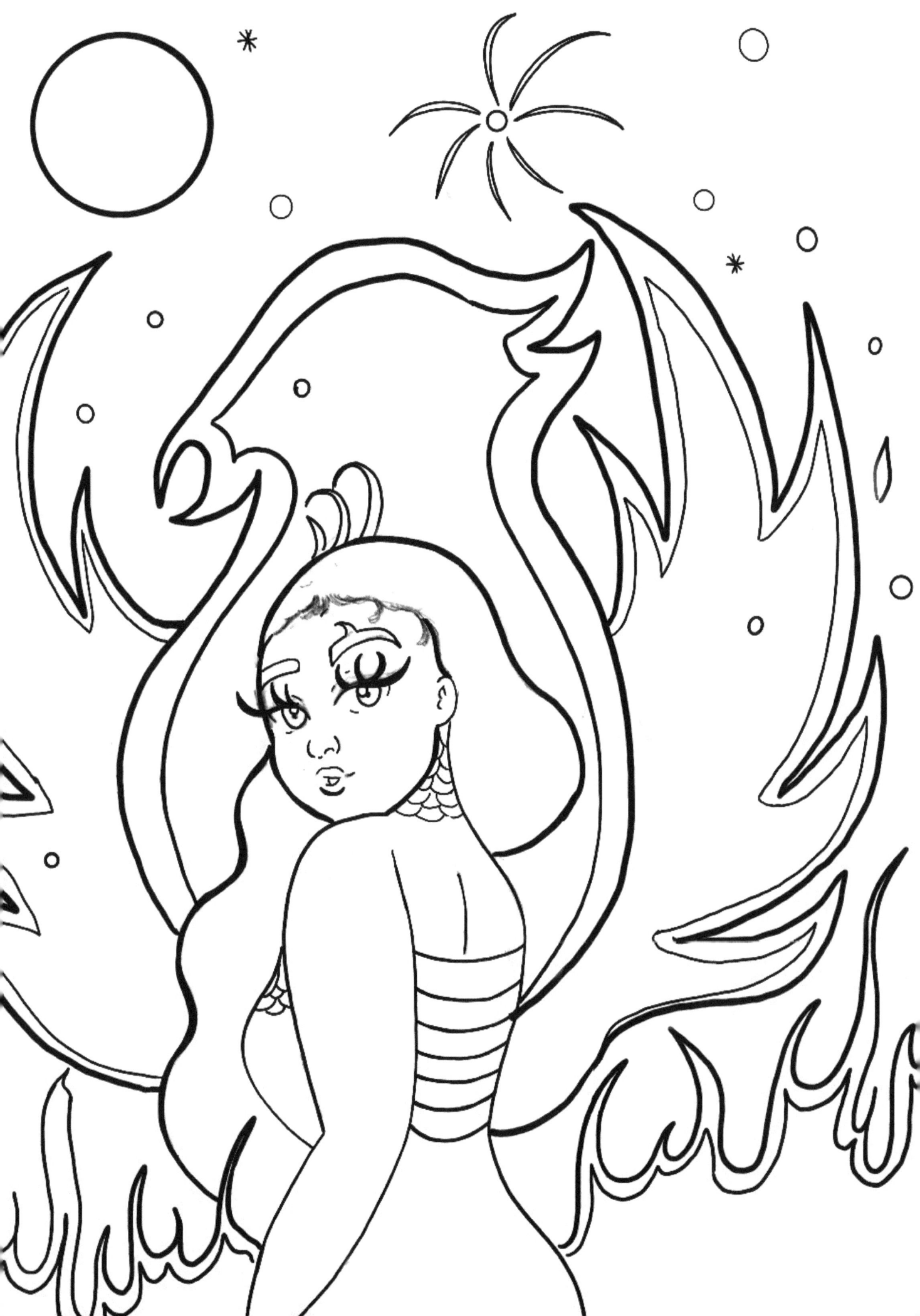

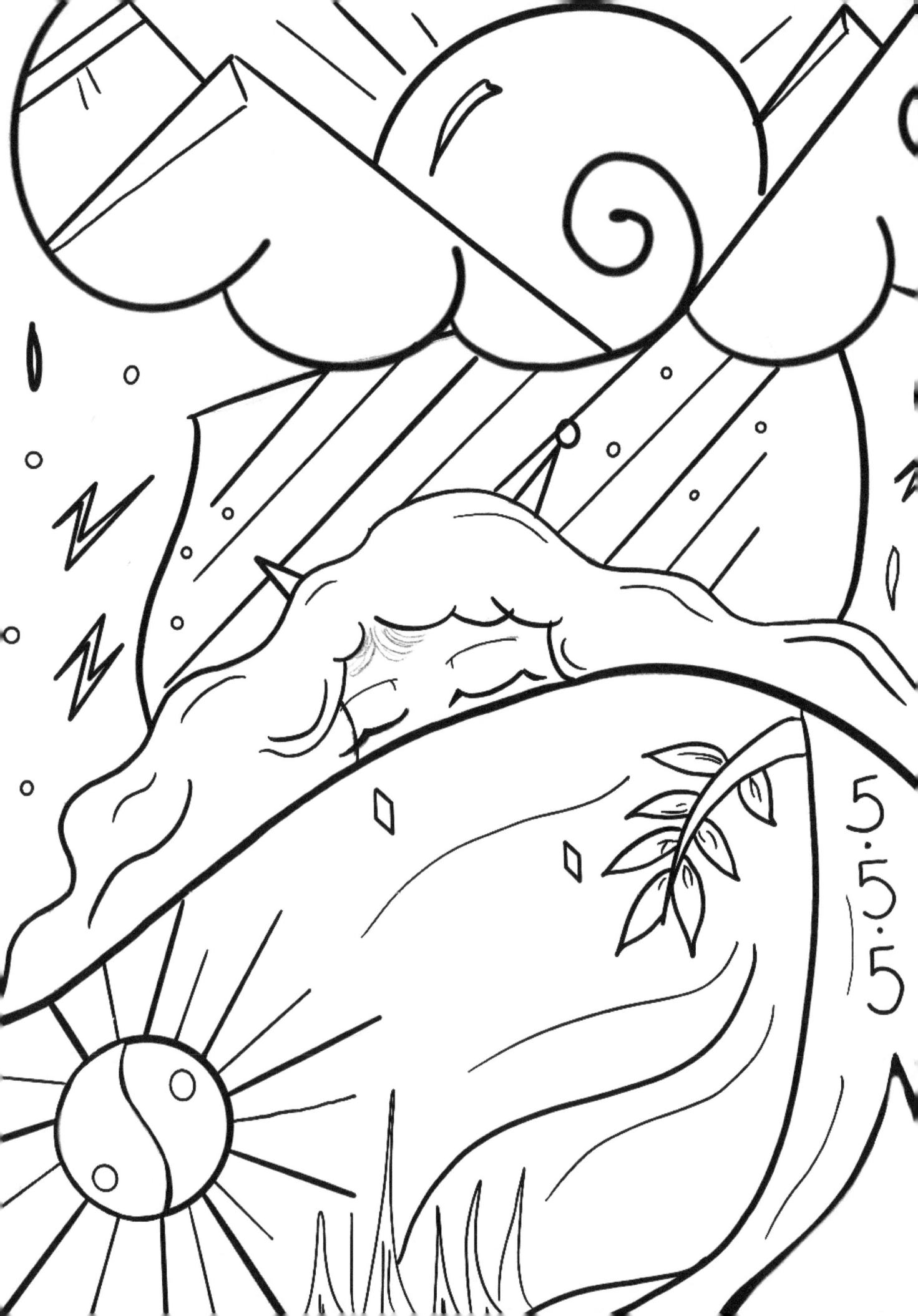

Let the world sleep on you while you dream big!

I am balanced

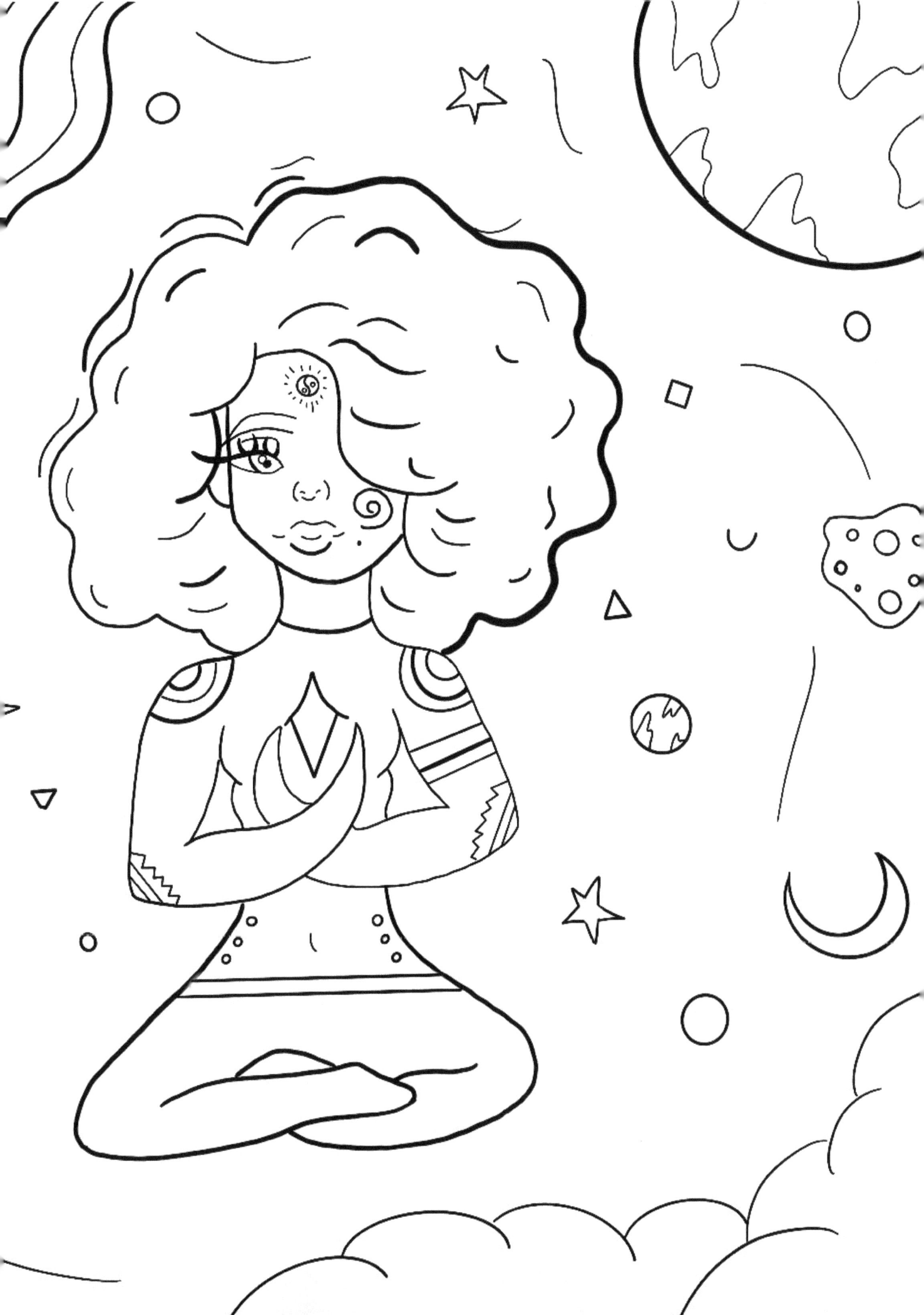

Love conquers all

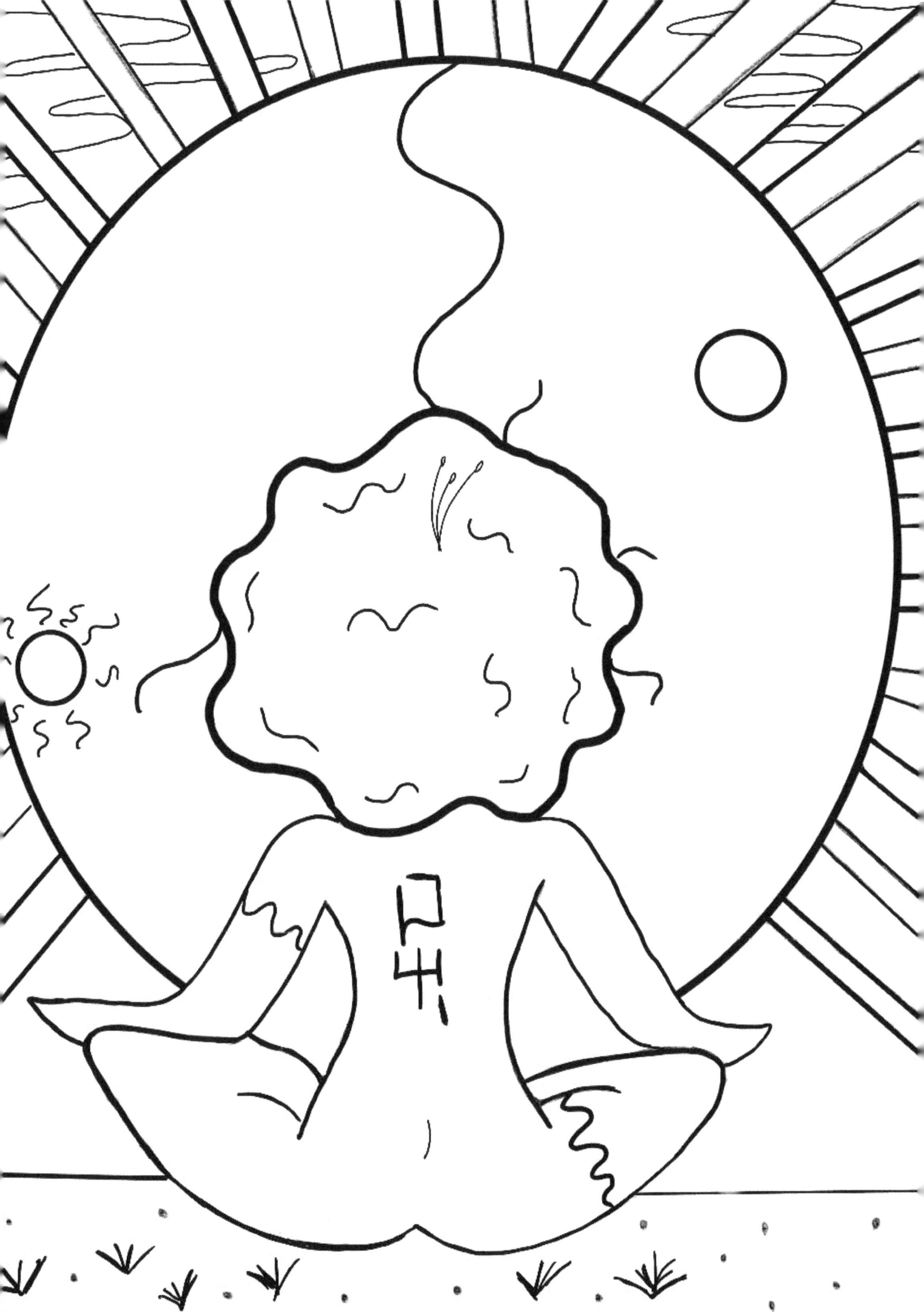

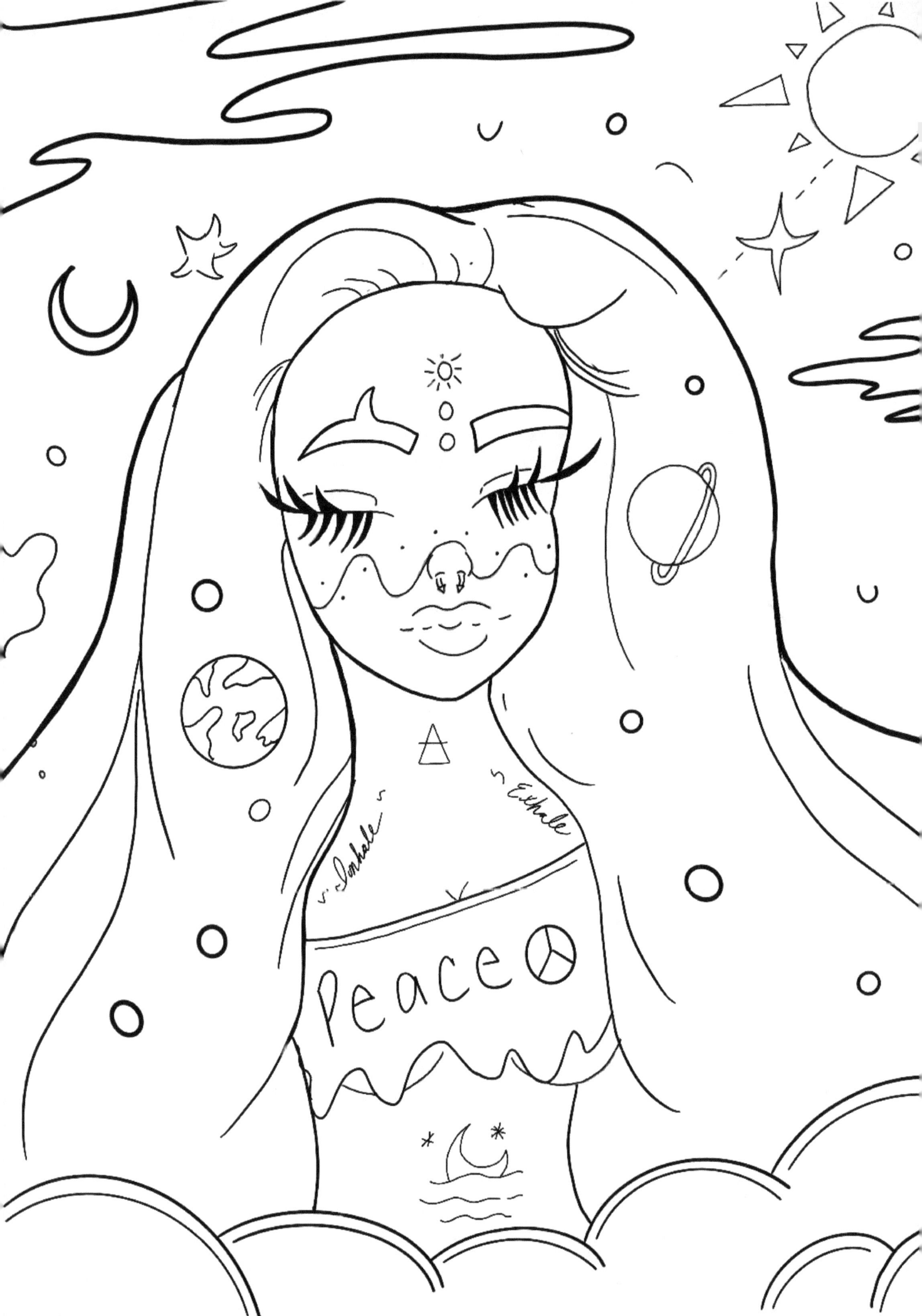

Tap into your superpower!

I create my own story!

☆

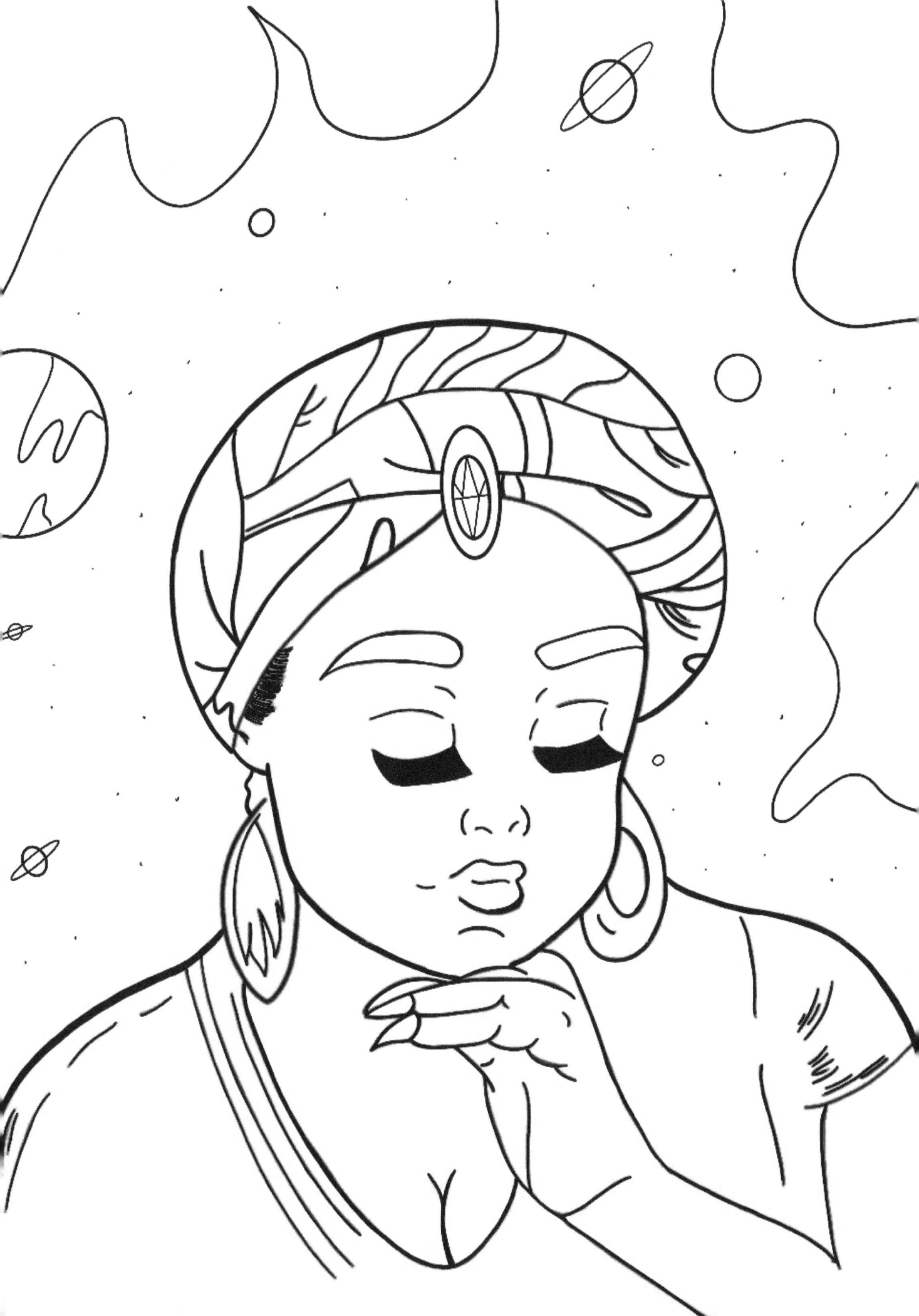

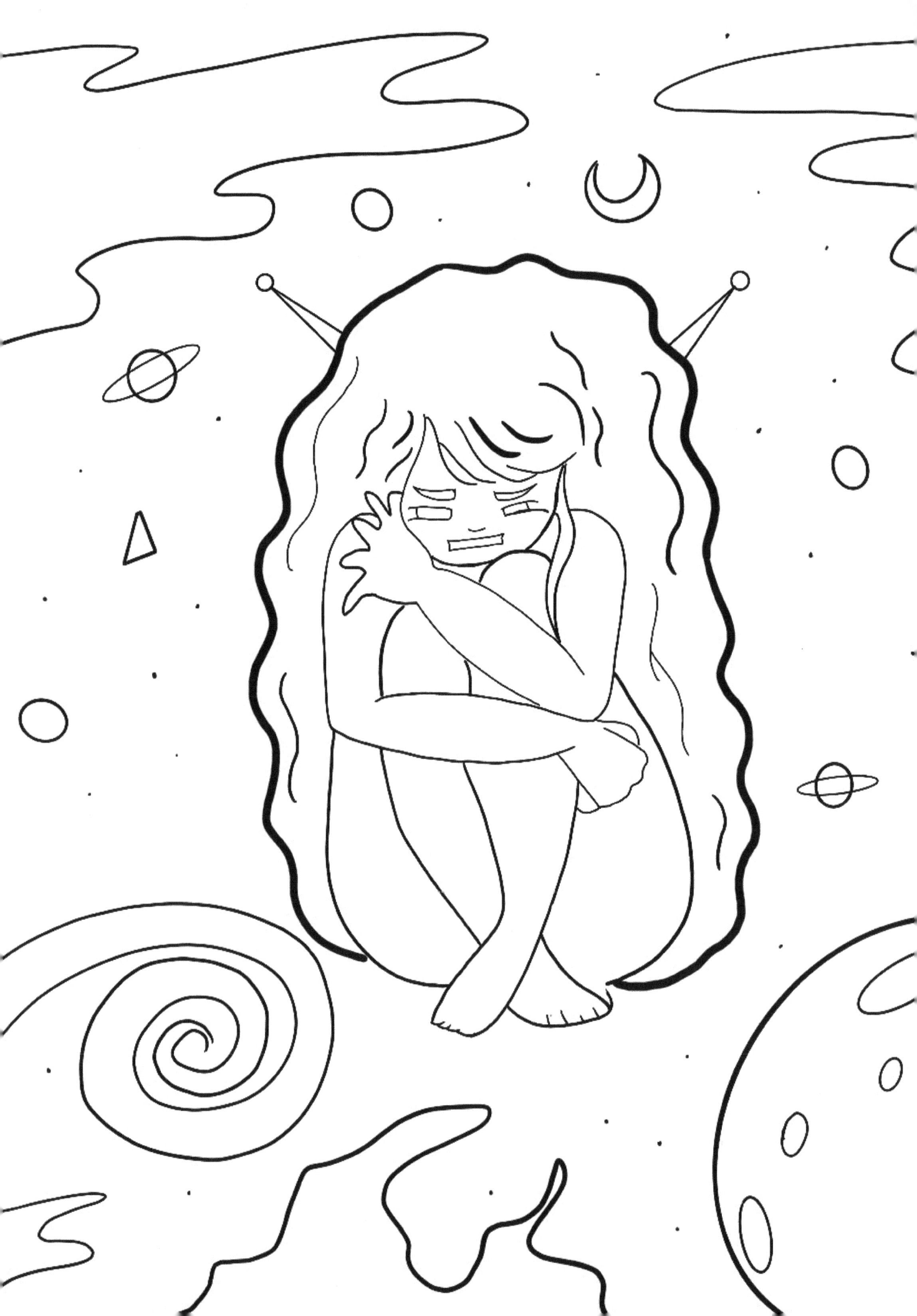

Break through hard times ☆

I am courageous!

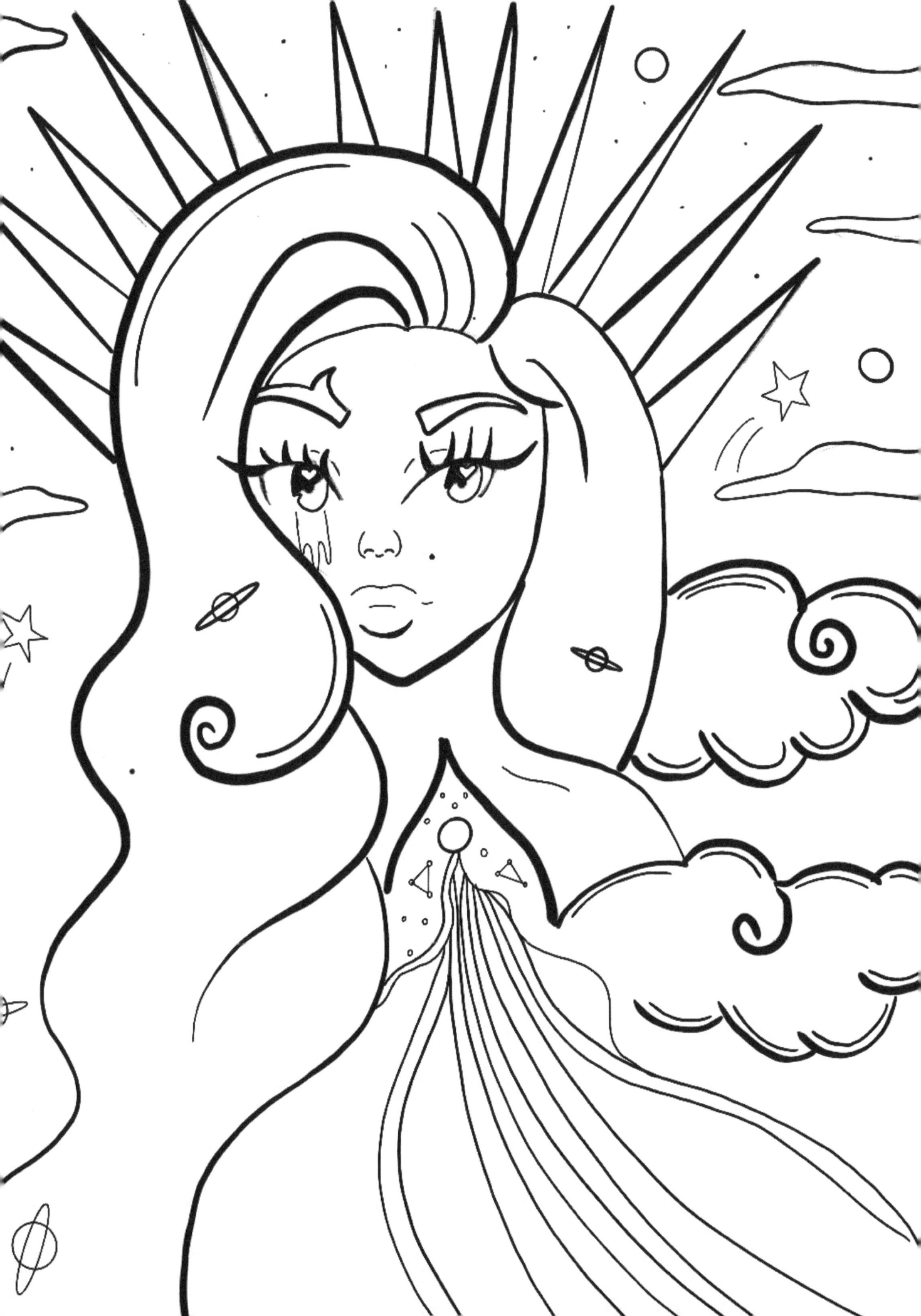

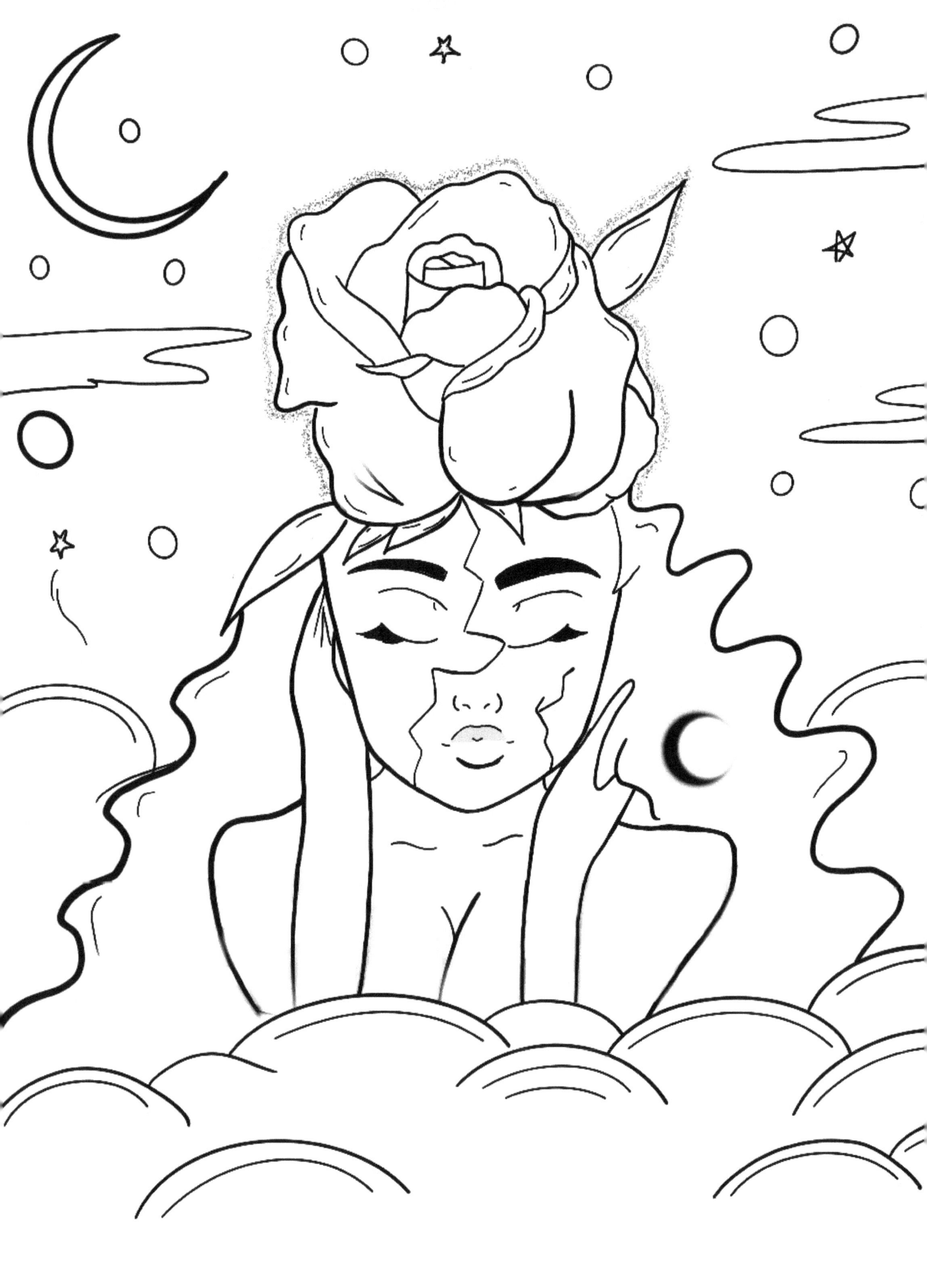

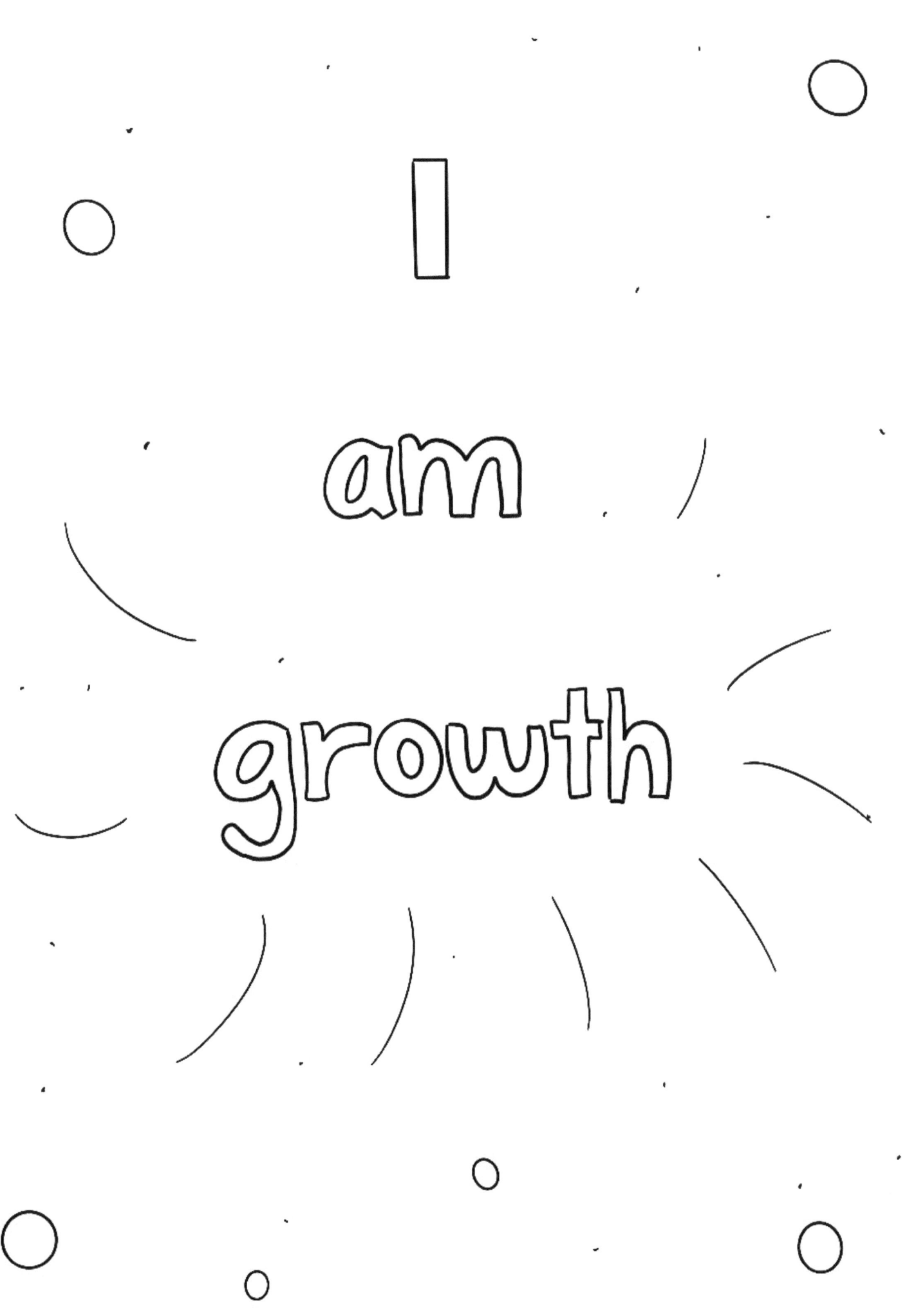

I am a star ☆

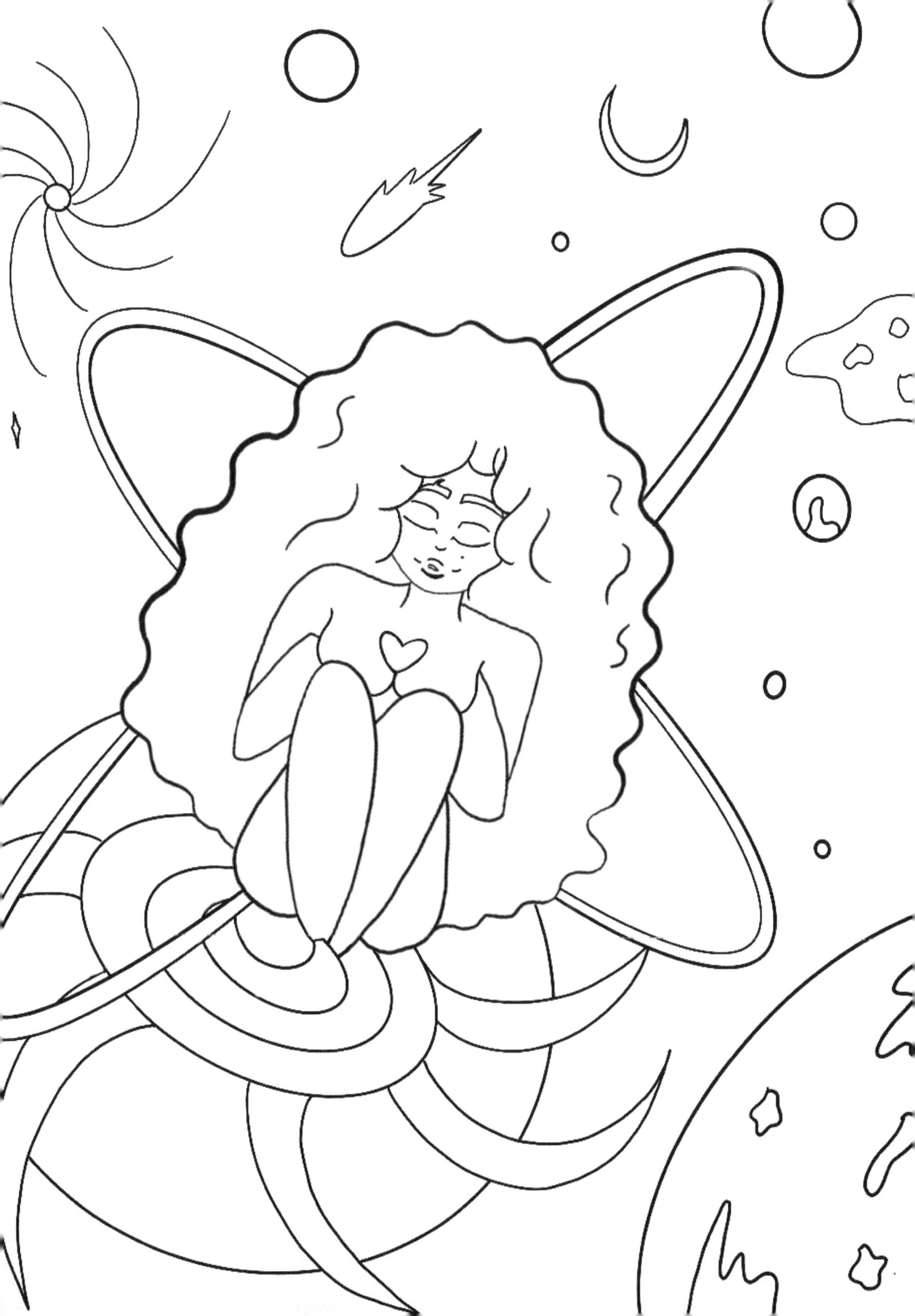

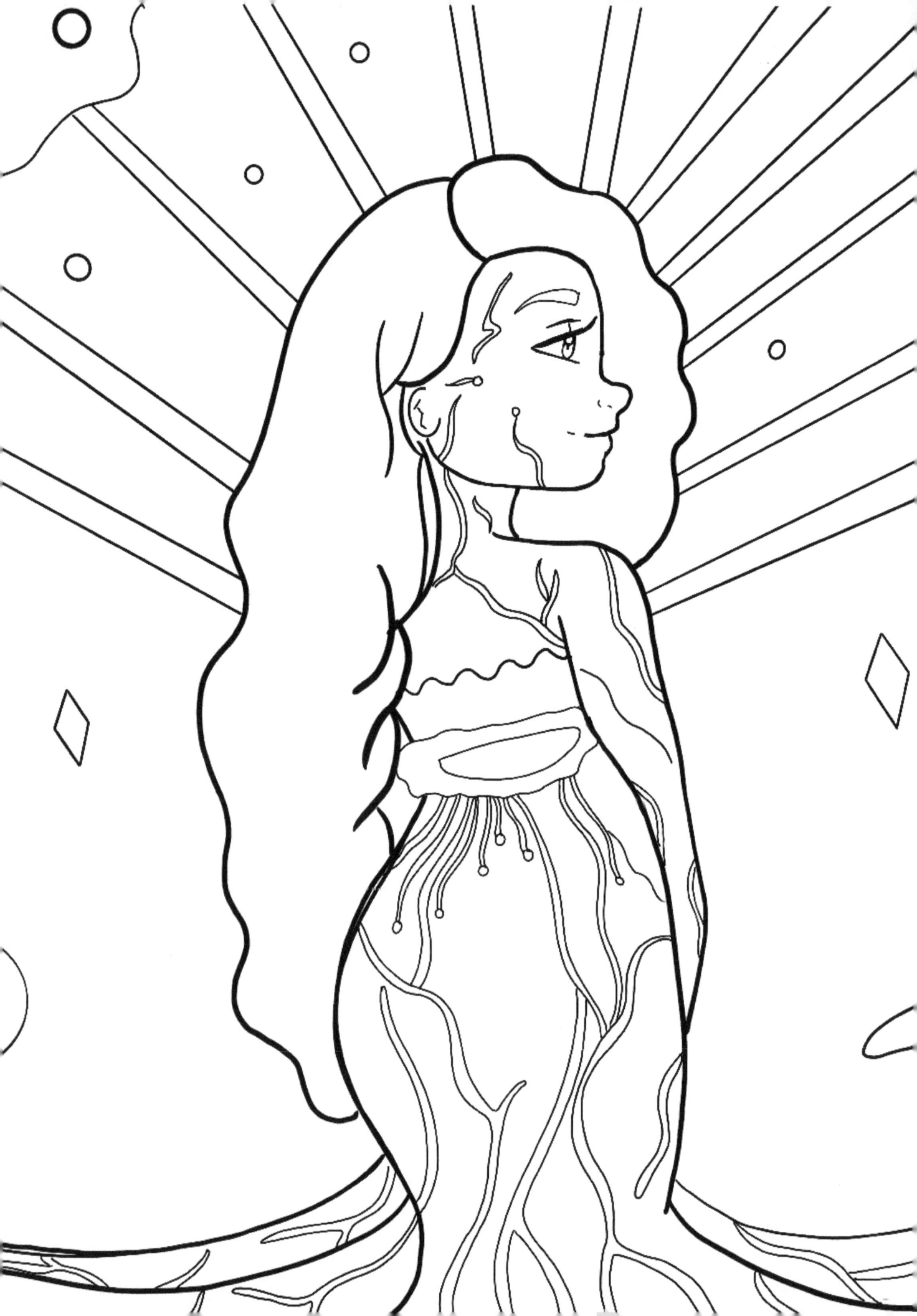

I am unstoppable !

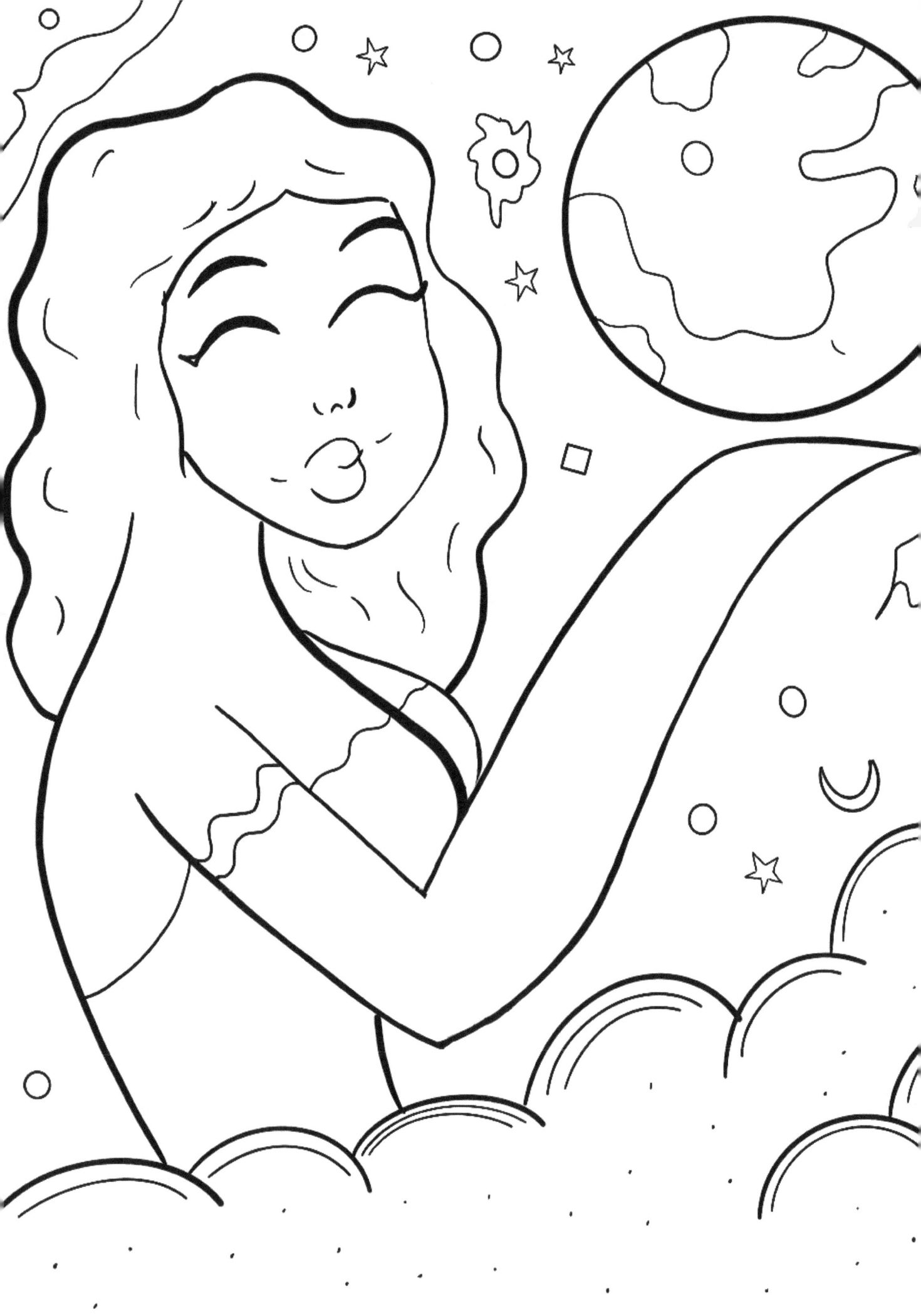

One person

an change

the world

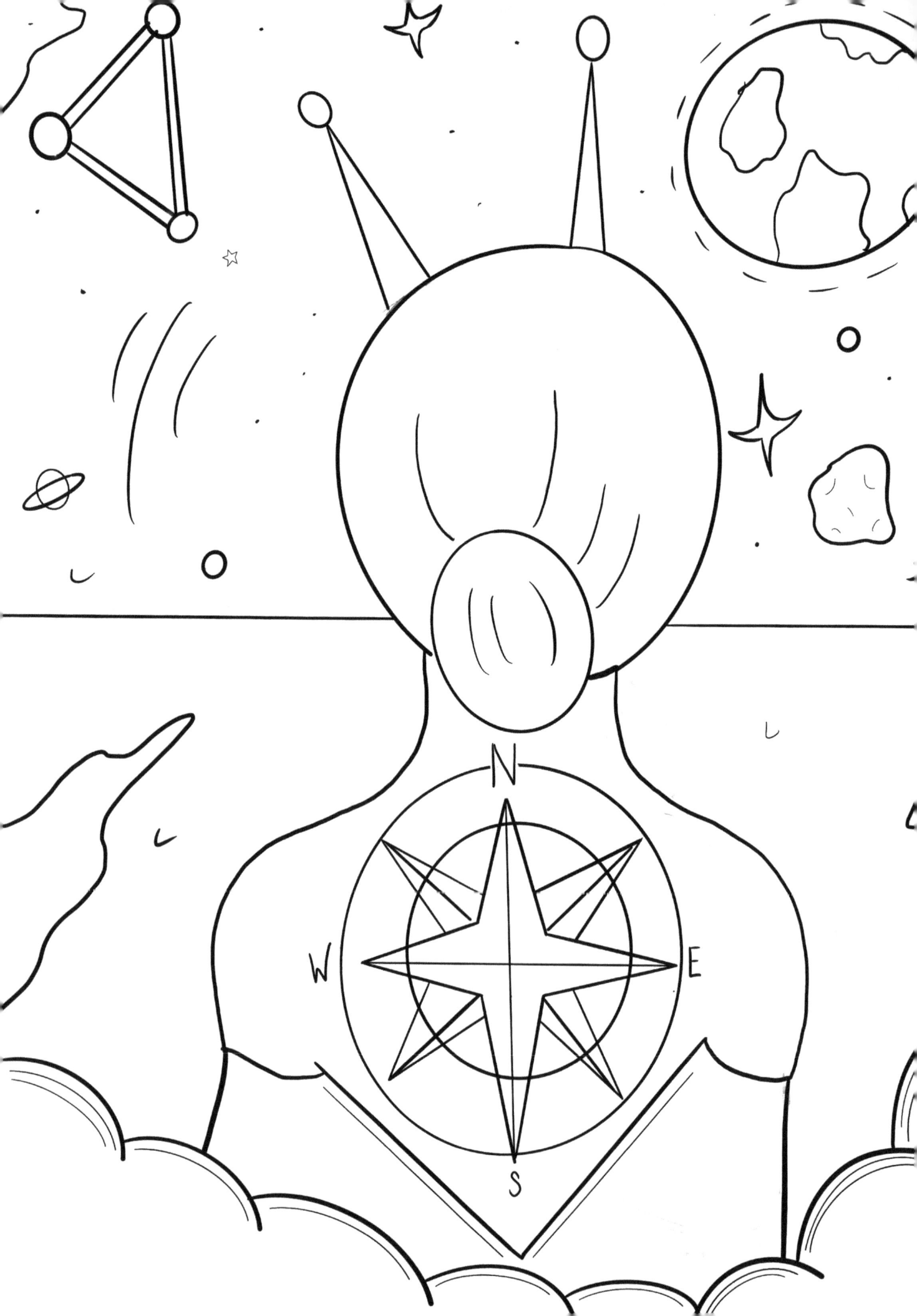

Following my inner compass

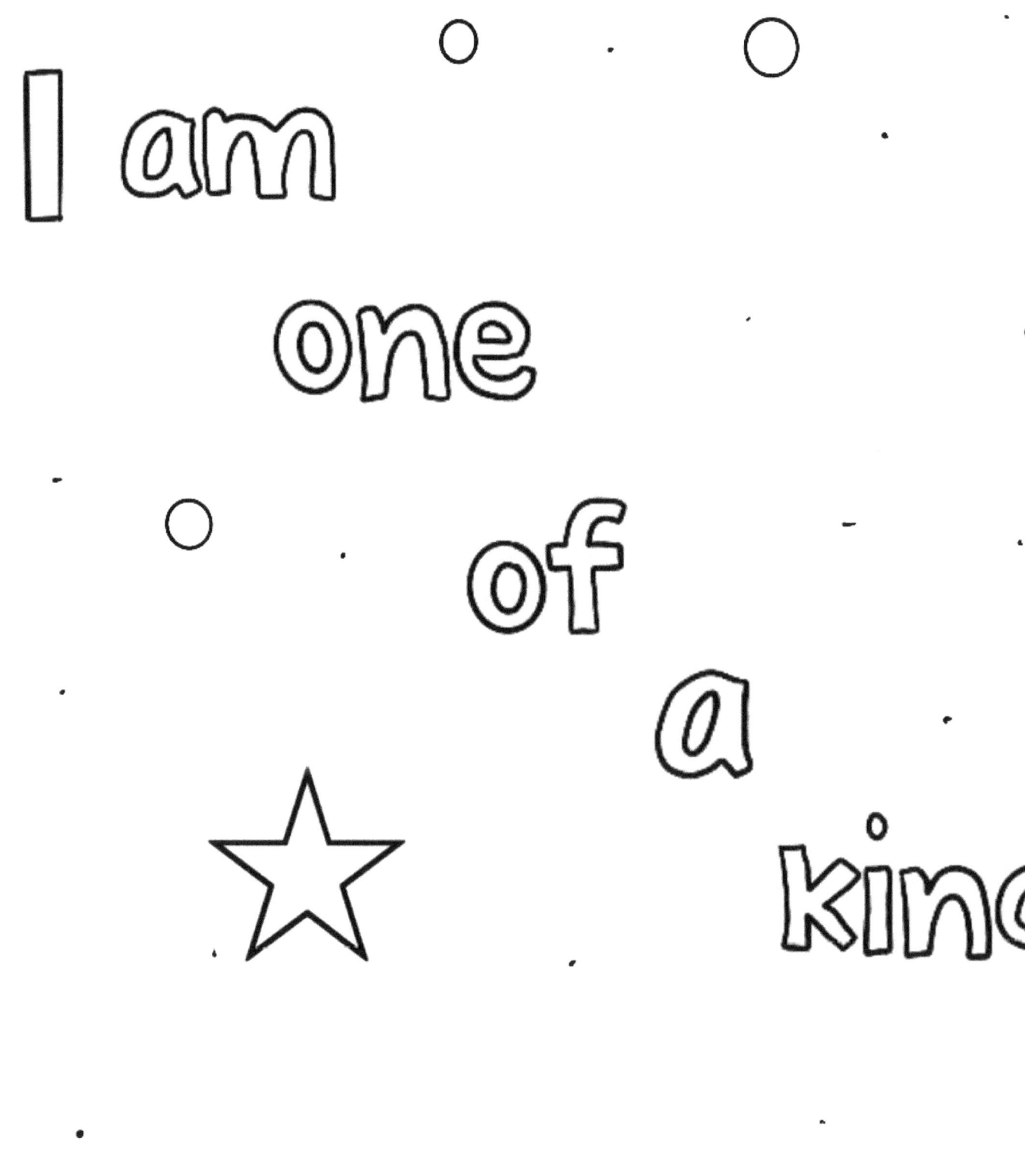

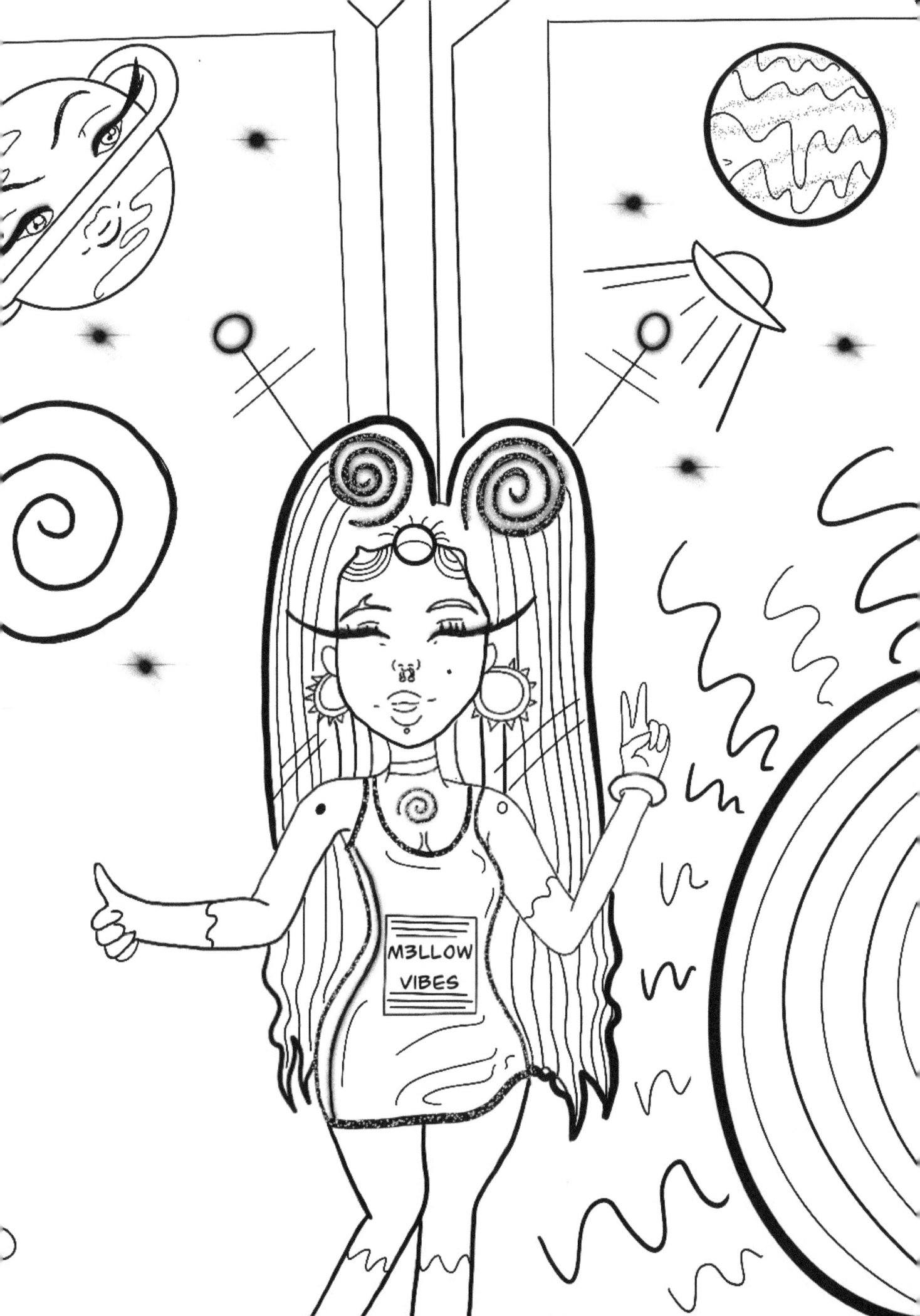

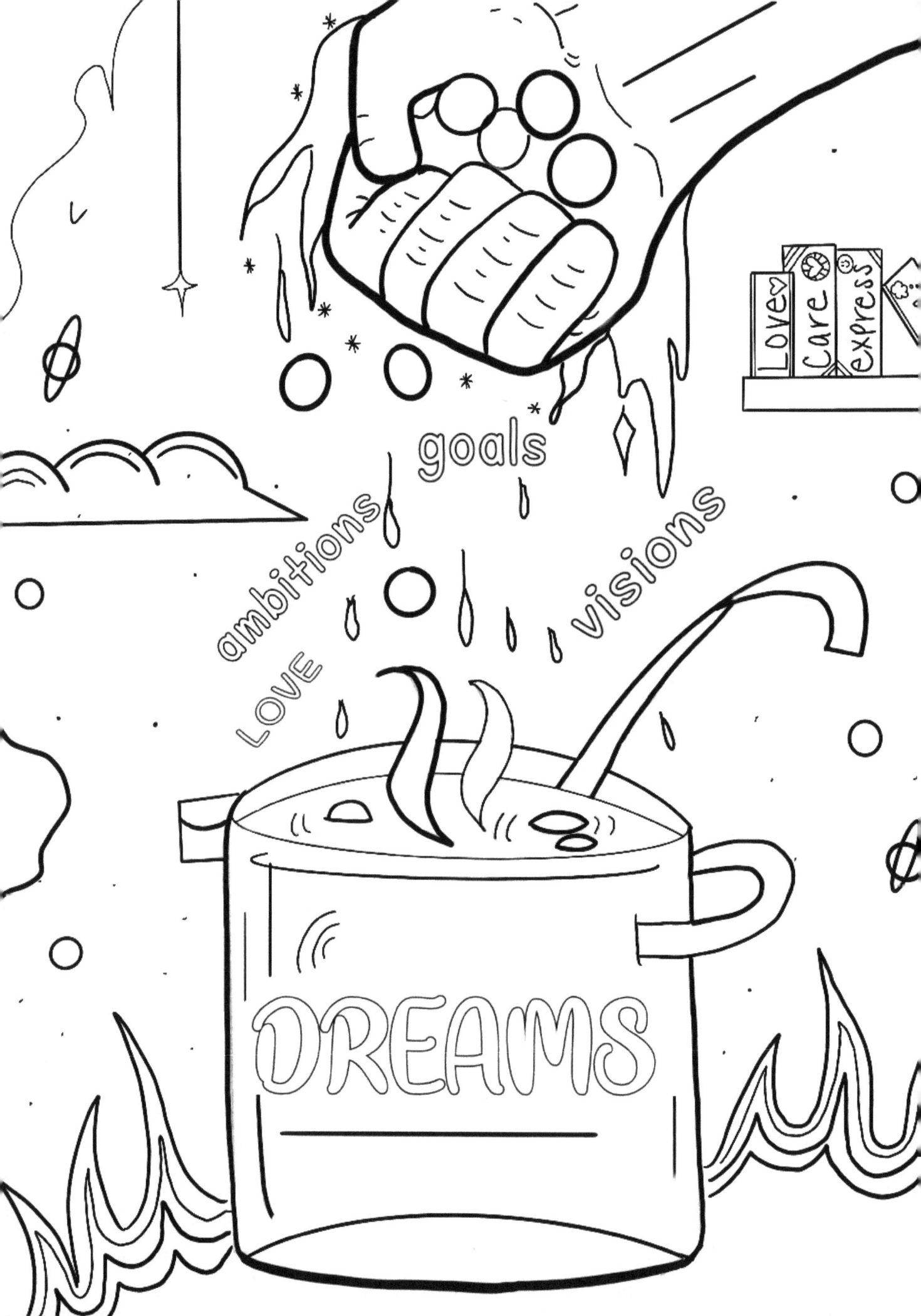

I am the main ingredient!

☆

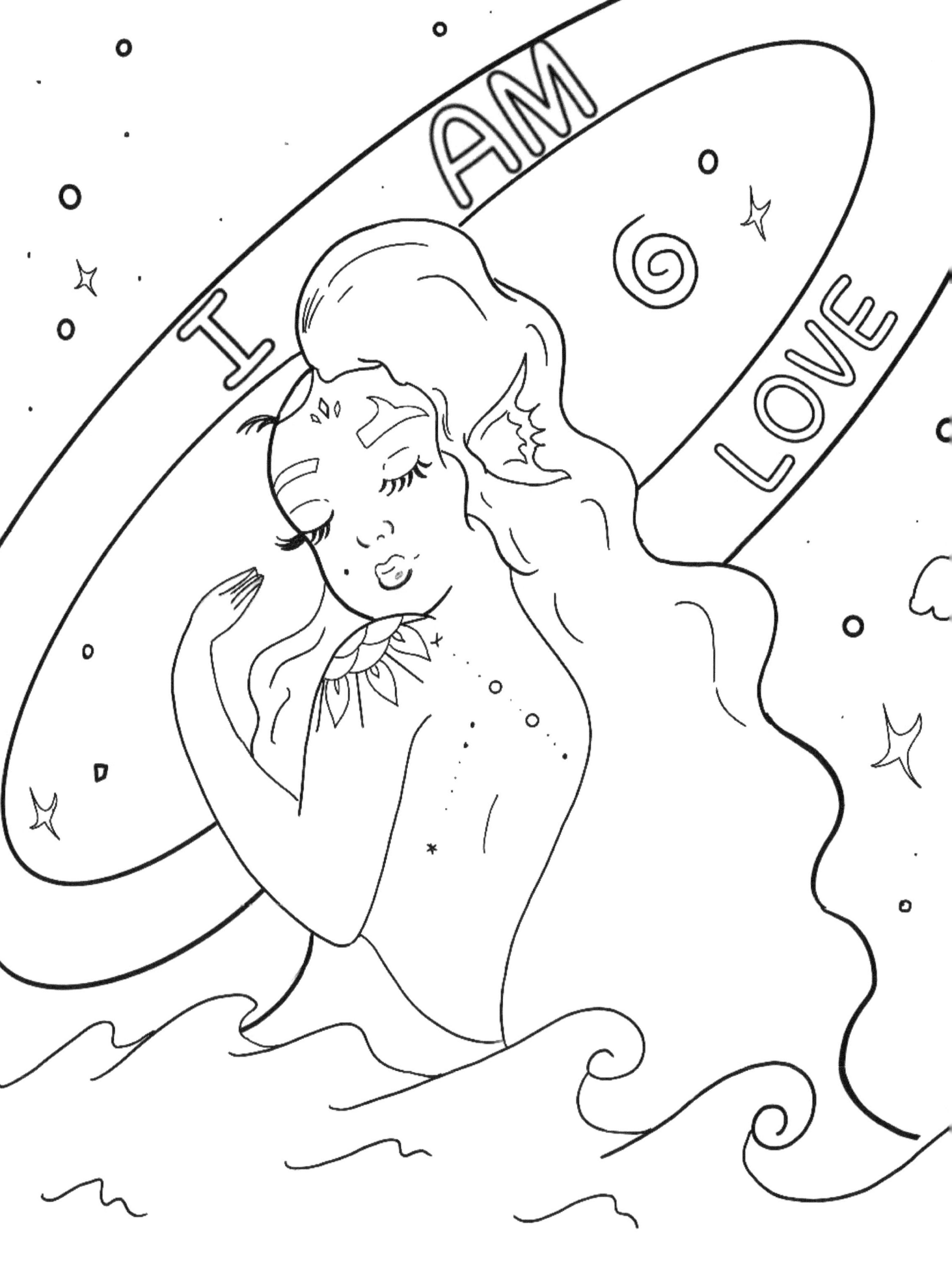

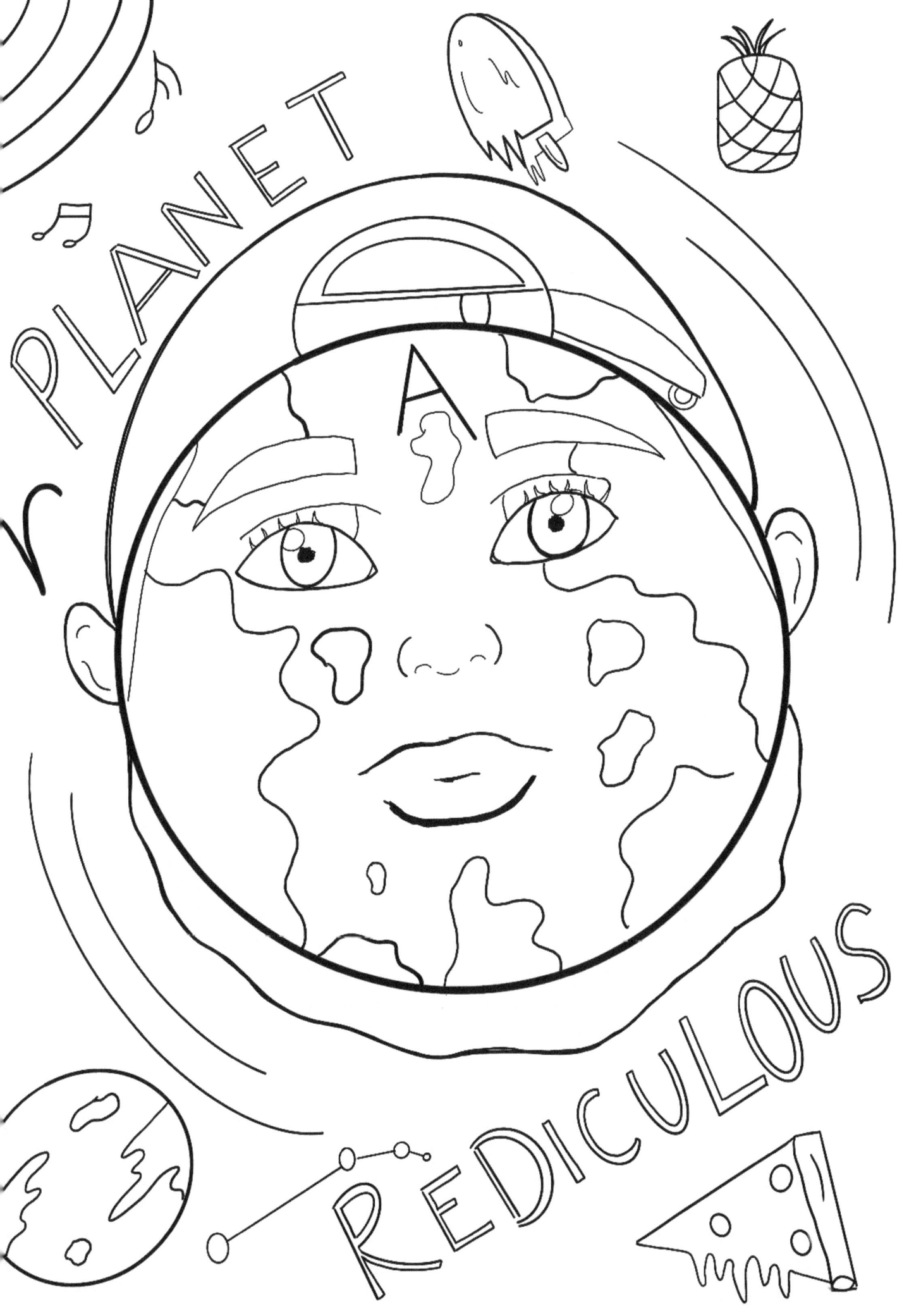

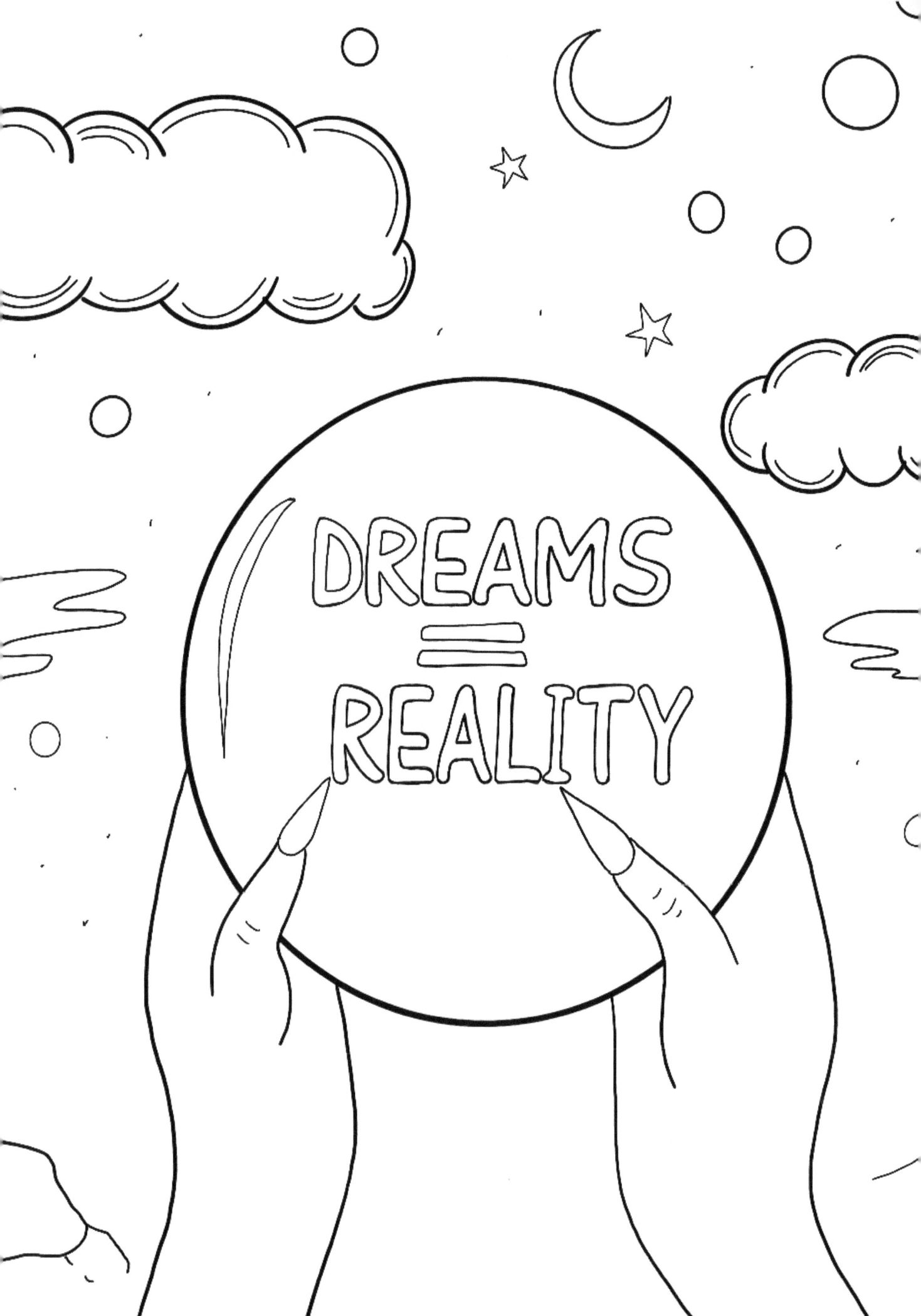

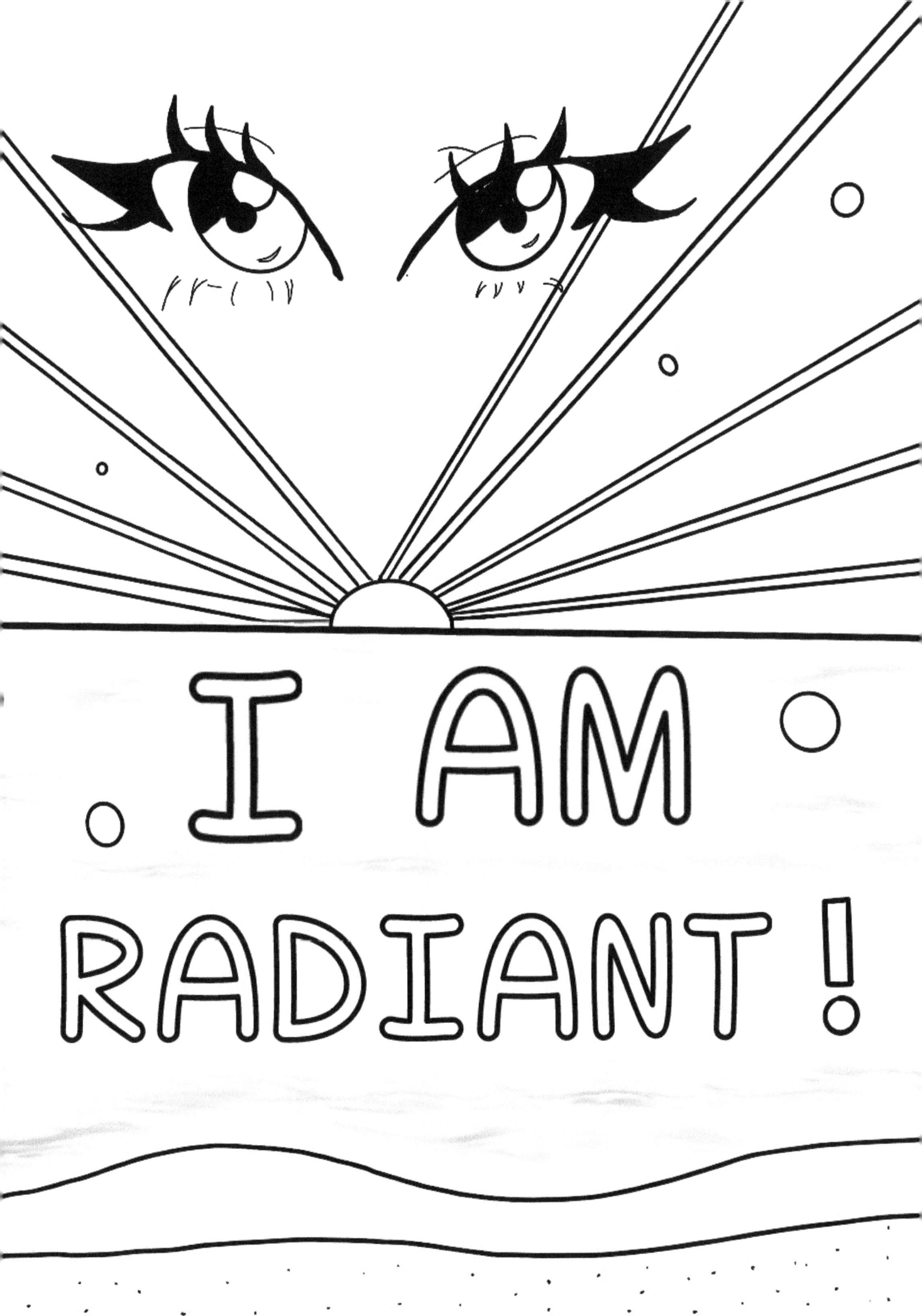

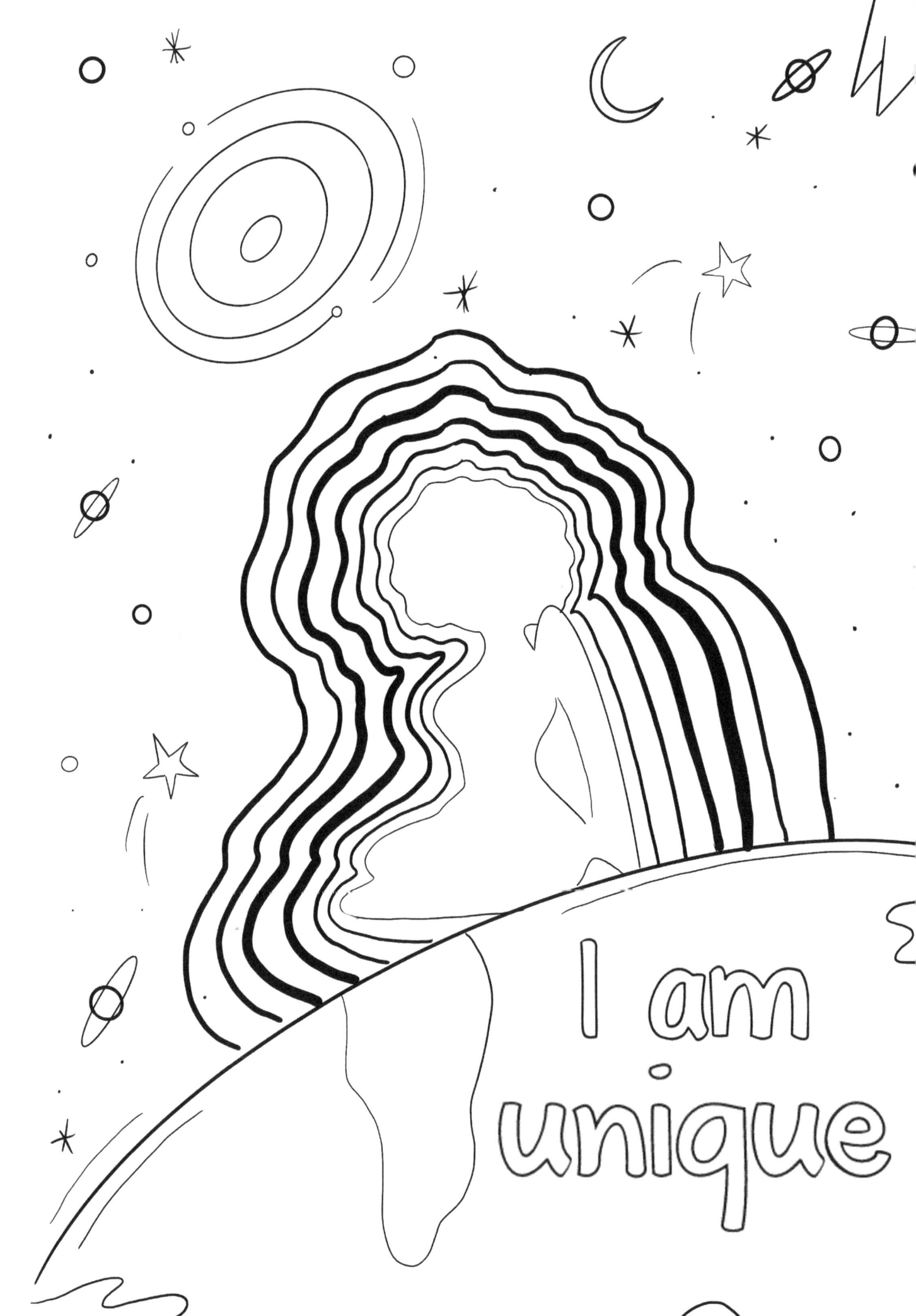

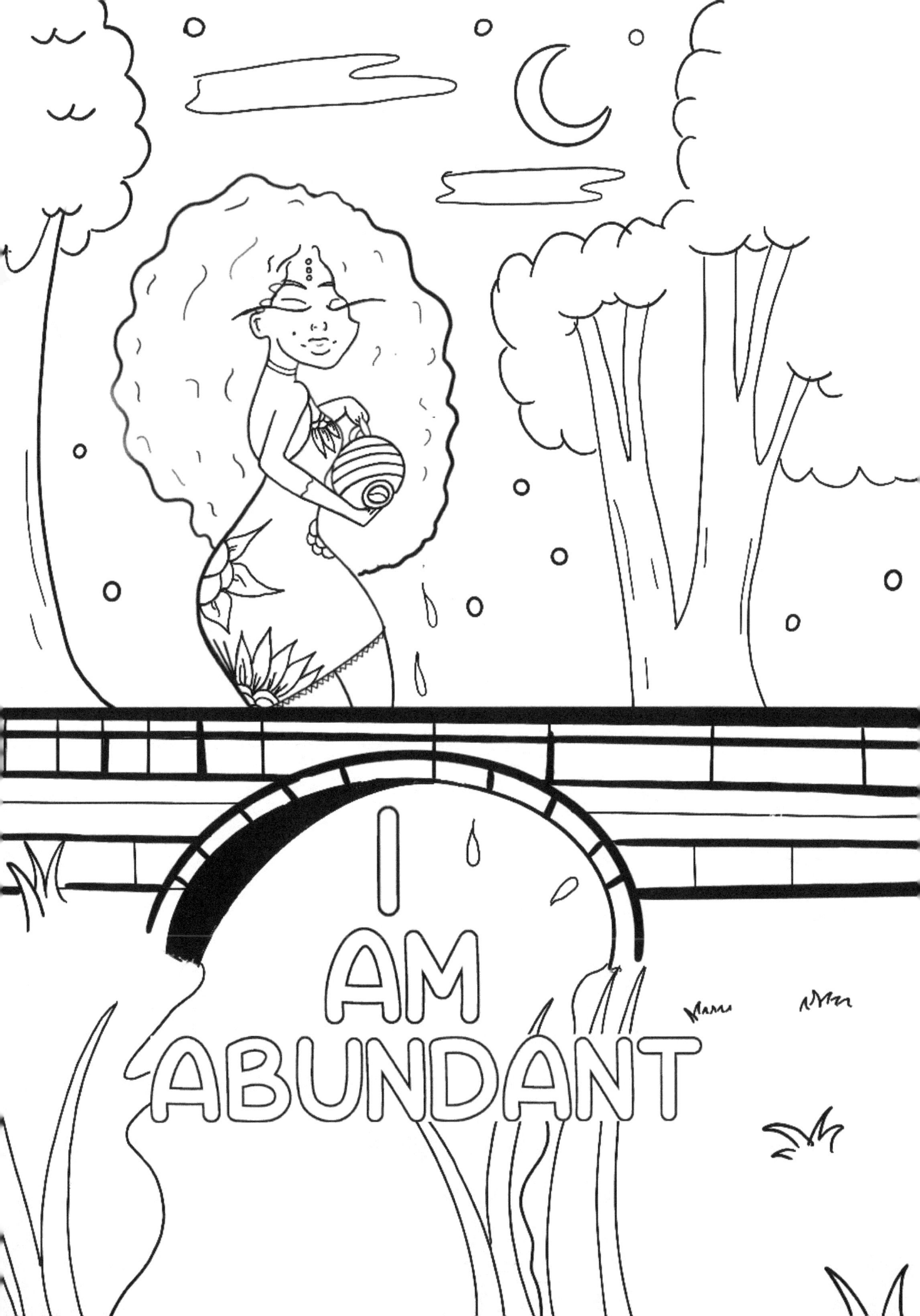

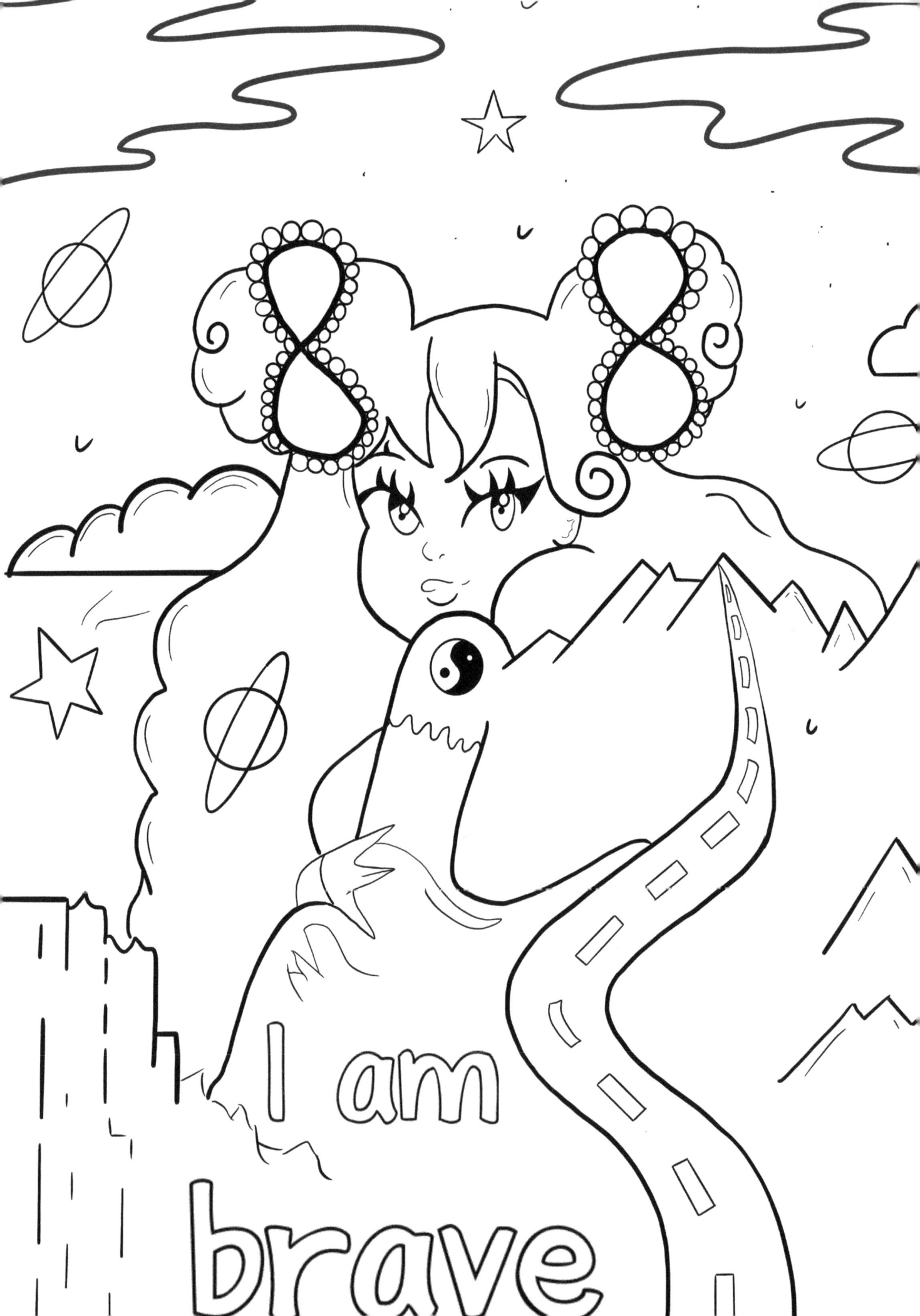

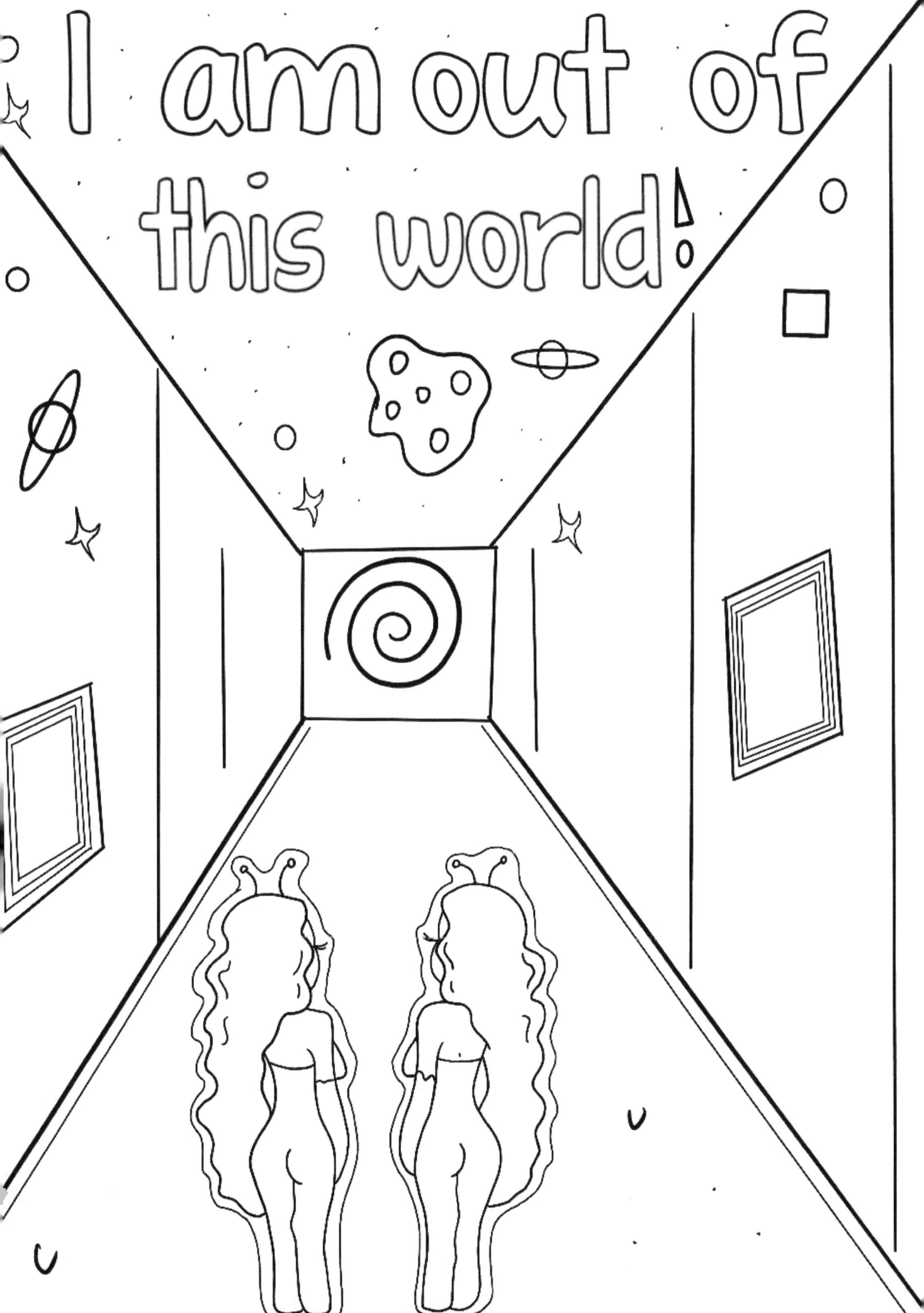

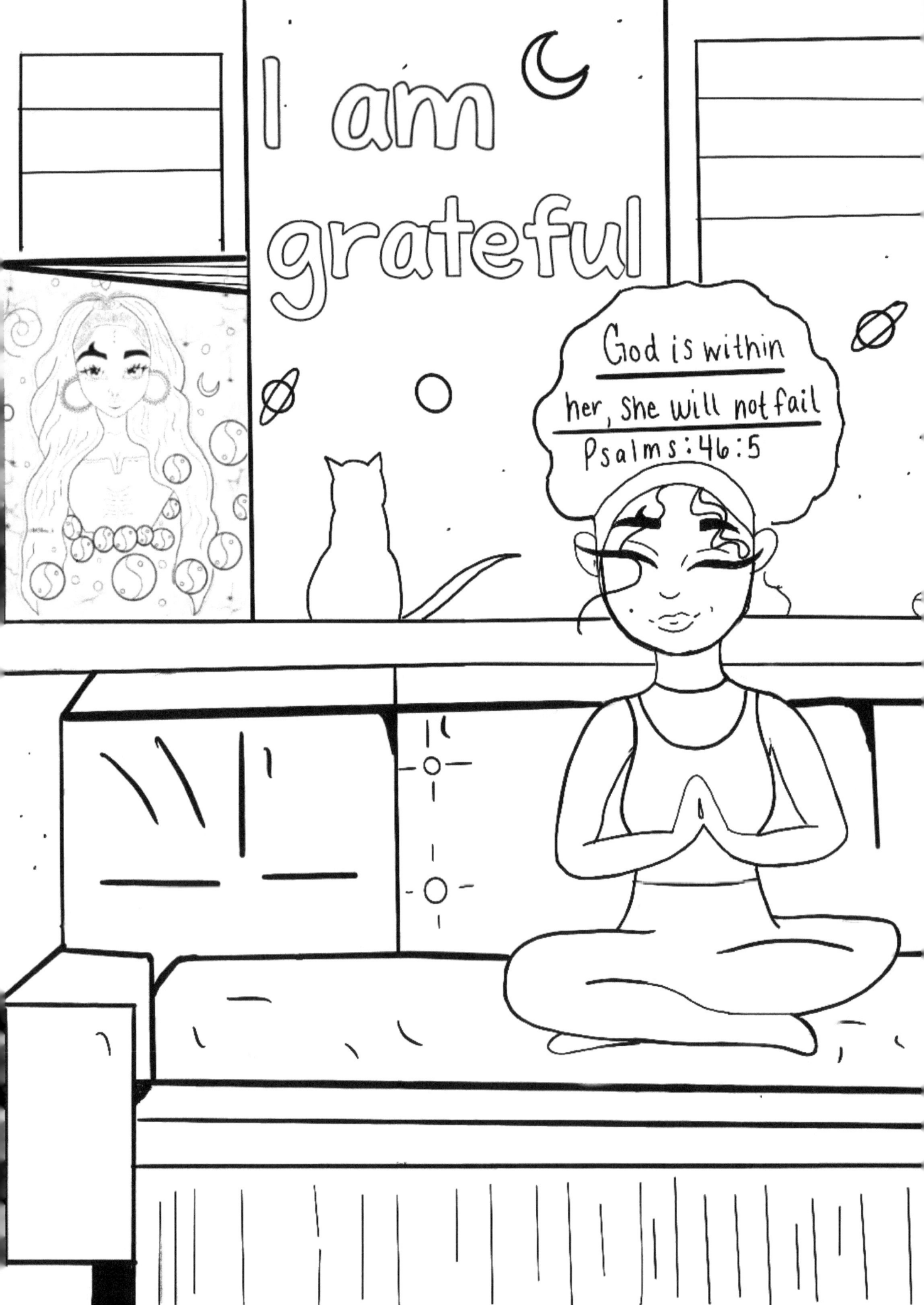

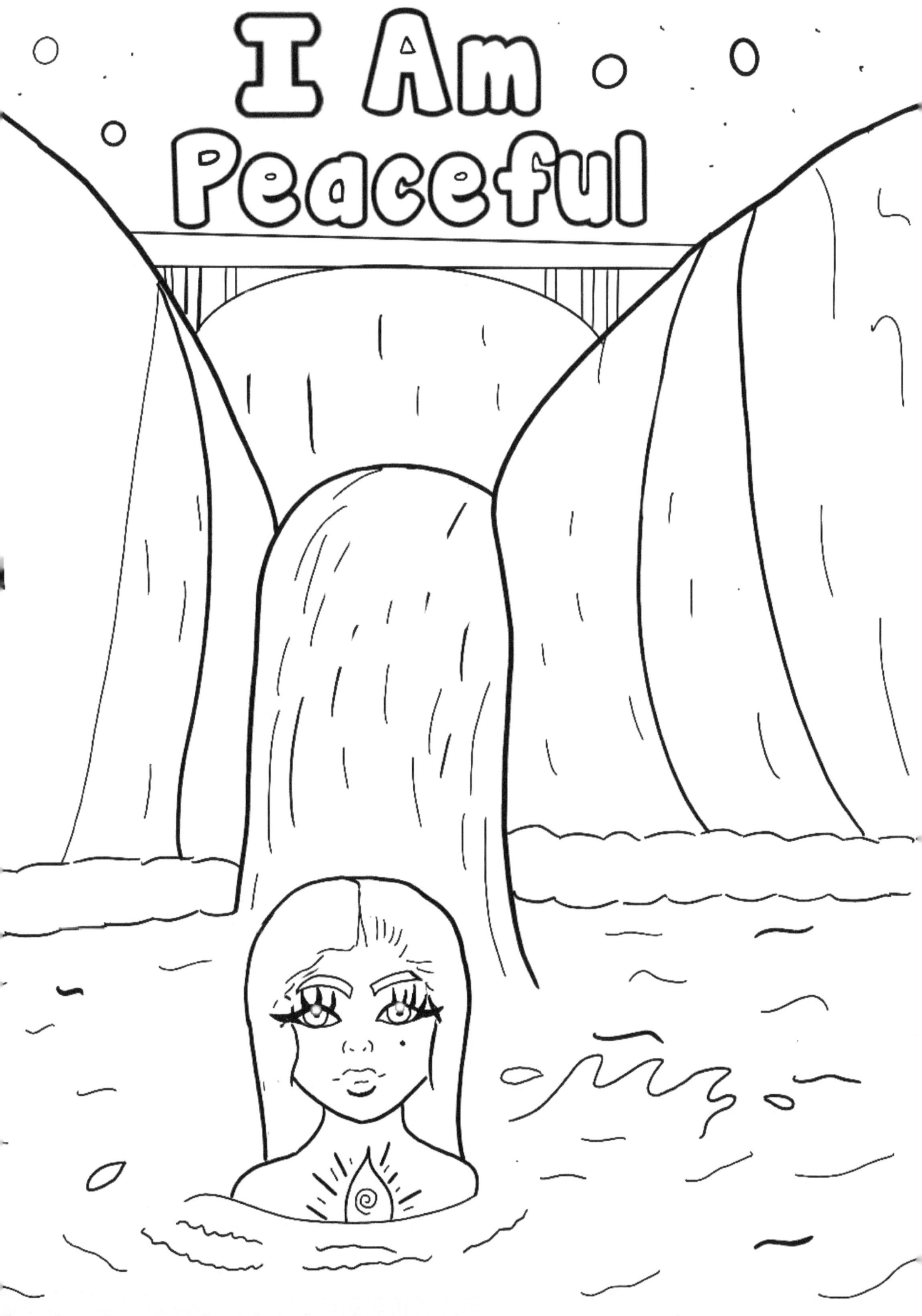

Hey lovebug! Have you ever had a passion or something of interest that you always wanted to pursue, but never had the courage to act upon it? Over the next few pages I would like for you to write down your dreams or goals that you would like to accomplish in life. Remember your time is now.

What are your dreams and goals?

Hey lovebugs! Enjoy the word search activity that I provided for you on the following page!

  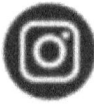  

@m3llow_k

```
H H S A U T H E N T I C O G O
E Y H T L A E H Y V L D D E R
S N O I S I V L T V L E A A A
R I D N Y G N I Z A M A E D S
E E L I H T O E U G A A T T O
V I C O N F I D E N T E D G F
T A R E V E R O D N I A D N I
Z A H O A E L E R H Y A H O L
E U T V A H T I A F R N C R E
N N P M D H E N H L F A I T A
N T S S E L R A E F I H R S N
T I S T L E Y S G A I T E C A
T H S S I H A E A N I R Y E F
O S L U S I N S T R E N G T H
S U P E R N O V A S U A A A E
```

AMAZING   AUTHENTIC   CONFIDENT   DREAMS
FAITH   FEARLESS   HEALTHY   LOVE
REALITY   STRENGTH   STRONG   SUPERNOVA
VISIONS

Instagram: @m3llow_k
TikTok: @m3llow_k
Facebook: @m3llow_k
Youtube: @m3llow_k
Twitter: m3llow_k

Please do not hesitate to tag @m3llow_k and share the artist in any
the coloring book's images or videos. The above list includes soci
media handles.

Hi, lovebug! Thank you for making it to the end of the coloring book! I hope you enjoyed the artwork and mini tivity! If you want to send fan mail our contact details are below!

M3llow_K
6608 Gulf Freeway South Ste 600
#128, La Marque, TX 77568

you haven't done so make sure to follow @m3llow_k on all social media to stay tuned into vibe M3llow_K Vibe!

Printed in the USA
CPSIA information can be obtained
at www.ICGtesting.com
LVHW061113220524
780860LV00020B/422